NINJA WOODFIRE GRILL & SMOKER COOKBOOK UK 2023

Elevate Your Grilling Game with Ninja Woodfire Electric BBQ Mouthwatering Recipes for Every Occasion.

AUTHOR: MATT P. BEAVEN

TABLE OF CONTENTS

INTRODUCTIONS

BRIEF EXPLANATION OF THE POPULARITY AND VERSATILITY OF WOODFIRE GRILLS AND SMOKERS

A Brief Overview of the Popularity and Versatility of Woodfire Grills and Smokers Woodfire barbecues and smokers have become incredibly popular among grill-masters and food connoisseurs in recent years. Food enthusiasts all around the world have fallen in love with them because of the smoky flavours and distinctive cooking experience they provide. Woodfire grills and smokers let you produce delectable dishes with that seductive smokey flavour using tender meats and fragrant vegetables. This cookbook is made to assist you in exploring a variety of culinary options and maximizing the capabilities of your Ninja Woodfire Grill and Smoker.

OVERVIEW OF THE AIM AND STRUCTURE OF THE COOKBOOK

The goal of the "Ninja Woodfire Outdoor Grill and Smoker Cookbook" is to provide you with a comprehensive guide to mastering the art of outdoor cooking with your Ninja Woodfire Grill and Smoker. This cookbook is jam-packed with delectable recipes, helpful hints, and practical techniques to help you up your grilling and smoking game.

The cookbook is laid out in an easy-to-follow format, beginning with basic information about the Ninja Woodfire Grill and Smoker, its features, and how to use it safely. It then delves into different recipe categories, such as grilling, smoking, roasting, baking, dehydrating, and reheating. Each recipe has been meticulously designed to ensure precise UK metric measurements, making it simple to follow along and achieve consistent results.

Whether you're a seasoned grill-master or just getting started, this cookbook will walk you through the steps of creating delectable dishes for any occasion. Prepare to wow your family and friends with a variety of recipes that highlight the versatility and power of the Ninja Woodfire Grill and Smoker.

Stay tuned as we embark on an exciting culinary adventure together, exploring the limitless possibilities that your Ninja Woodfire Grill and Smoker offers!

THE ART OF WOODFIRE COOKING

EXPLORING THE HISTORY AND TRADITION BEHIND WOODFIRE GRILLING AND SMOKING

Exploring the history and tradition behind woodfire grilling and smoking Woodfire cooking has a long and illustrious history. It's a technique that cultures all over the world have embraced, from ancient civilizations to modern-day barbecue enthusiasts. In this chapter, we'll look at the history and evolution of woodfire grilling and smoking, as well as the traditional methods and techniques that have influenced how we cook with fire. Discover the fascinating stories and cultural influences that have contributed to the longevity of woodfire cooking as a culinary tradition.

UNDERSTANDING THE BENEFITS OF USING A NINJA WOODFIRE GRILL AND SMOKER

A multifunctional cooking tool that brings the art of woodfire cooking to your backyard is the Ninja Woodfire Grill and Smoker. We'll talk about the special qualities and benefits of using a Ninja Woodfire Grill and Smoker in this section. This grill and smoker combination offer a number of advantages that improve your cooking experience, from its precise temperature control to its cutting-edge design. Examine the benefits of using wood as a fuel source, the efficiency of a multipurpose cooking appliance, and the ability to achieve both high-heat grilling and low-and-slow smoking.

You'll develop a greater appreciation for the artistry and technique involved in producing exceptional grilled and smoked foods by learning about the background and customs of woodfire cooking as well as the specific advantages of the Ninja Woodfire Grill and Smoker. Prepare to honour the tradition of cooking over a fire and use the Ninja Woodfire Grill and Smoker to up your outdoor cooking game.

GETTING STARTED

ESSENTIAL TOOLS AND EQUIPMENT FOR SUCCESSFUL WOODFIRE COOKING

You must have the proper tools and supplies on hand before starting your woodfire cooking journey with the Ninja Woodfire Grill and Smoker. We'll walk you through the necessary supplies in this chapter to make sure your cooking experience is seamless. We'll go over everything you need to set up your outdoor kitchen for successful woodfire cooking, from grilling tools and thermometers to wood selection and fire starters. Learn about the essential equipment that will enable you to produce consistently delicious grilled and smoked dishes.

SAFETY TIPS AND PRECAUTIONS FOR A SECURE COOKING ENVIRONMENT

To protect yourself, your loved ones, and your property while cooking with fire, it's essential to establish a secure cooking environment. We'll give you helpful safety advice and recommendations in this section for using the Ninja Woodfire Grill and Smoker. We'll go over the crucial safety precautions that will give you peace of mind while you embark on your woodfire cooking adventures, from setting up a safe cooking area to handling hot surfaces and managing fire hazards. By putting safety first, you can take pleasure in cooking without risking your health.

You'll be ready to get the most out of your Ninja Woodfire Grill and Smoker by being aware of the necessary tools and equipment for woodfire cooking and taking safety precautions. You'll be prepared to explore the wide variety of recipes and techniques that are waiting for you in the following chapters if you have the right tools and keep safety in mind.

TYPES OF WOOD AND CHARCOAL

OVERVIEW OF DIFFERENT TYPES OF WOOD AND THEIR IMPACT ON FLAVOUR

The distinctive flavour that each type of wood adds to food is one of the distinguishing features of woodfire cooking. We'll look at the various kinds of wood used frequently in the UK for grilling and smoking in this chapter. Each type of wood, from hardwoods like oak and hickory to fruitwoods like apple and cherry, adds a distinct flavour and aroma to your food. We'll go into detail about each type of wood and describe how it can enhance the flavours of your grilled and smoked creations. You can select the ideal wood to improve the flavour of your recipes by being aware of the effects of various wood types.

CHOOSING THE RIGHT WOOD OR CHARCOAL FOR SPECIFIC RECIPES

In terms of woodfire cooking, choosing the appropriate wood or charcoal for a particular recipe can have a big impact on how it turns out. We'll walk you through the process of selecting the right wood or charcoal based on the flavours you want to achieve in this section. We'll offer suggestions on which wood or charcoal pairs best with various types of meats, vegetables, and even desserts, depending on whether you're going for a robust and smoky profile or a milder and subtler taste. Using the Ninja Woodfire Grill and Smoker, you'll be able to produce dishes of the highest number with the help of our professional advice.

MASTERING THE TECHNIQUES

STEP-BY-STEP INSTRUCTIONS ON USING THE NINJA WOODFIRE GRILL AND SMOKER

We'll go over precise, step-by-step instructions for using the Ninja Woodfire Grill and Smoker in this chapter. We'll walk you through the entire process, from setting up the grill for cooking to comprehending the various features and functions. You'll discover the proper techniques for lighting the fire, managing the airflow, and preparing the grill for both direct and indirect cooking. You will feel comfortable using your Ninja Woodfire Grill and Smoker like a pro after reading our easy-to-understand directions and helpful advice.

CONTROLLING TEMPERATURE AND MANAGING HEAT ZONES FOR OPTIMAL RESULTS

When it comes to getting your dishes just the right amount of doneness and flavour, temperature control is essential. To ensure precise and consistent cooking, we'll show you how to regulate the temperature on your Ninja Woodfire Grill and Smoker in this section. You'll discover how to establish and control heat zones so you can perfectly sear, grill, and smoke your ingredients. We'll go over methods for adjusting the temperature based on the demands of the recipe, whether you're searing at high heat or cooking slowly. With our assistance, you'll be able to master the art of cooking and produce superb results each and every time.

TIPS FOR ACHIEVING THE PERFECT SEAR, SMOKE, AND TENDERNESS IN YOUR DISHES

For the best grilled and smoked dishes, it's crucial to master the techniques for searing, smoking, and getting tender results. In this section, we'll share our insider advice on how to sear meats to perfection, give them a delicious smoky flavour, and keep them tender and juicy. We'll talk about things like the value of preheating, how to arrange ingredients properly, how to add smoke flavour with wood chips or chunks, and how to get tender meat. With the help of our insider advice, you'll be able to elevate your woodfire cooking to a whole new level and wow your loved ones with mouth-watering flavours.

RECITES

SMOKER

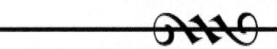

BRISKET WITH TANGY BBQ SAUCE

Prep Time 15 minutes	Cooking Time 5 hours	Servings 5

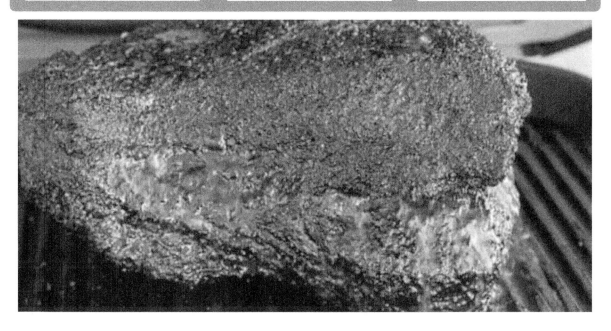

INGREDIENTS:

- 1.5 kg beef brisket
- 40 ml olive oil
- 1 tbsp paprika
- 1 tbsp brown sugar
- 1 tsp salt
- 1 tsp black pepper

- 1/2 tsp garlic powder
- 1/2 tsp onion powder
- 1/2 tsp cayenne pepper
- 200 ml beef broth
- 250 ml BBQ sauce

TANGY BBQ SAUCE:

- 150 ml ketchup
- 40 ml apple cider vinegar
- 1 tbsp Worcestershire sauce
- 1 tbsp brown sugar
- 1 tbsp Dijon mustard

- 1/2 tsp smoked paprika
- 1/2 tsp garlic powder
- 1/2 tsp onion powder
- Salt and pepper to taste

INSTRUCTIONS:

1. Preheat the Ninja Woodfire Grill and Smoker to 110°C with the smoker function.

2. To make the dry rub, combine paprika, brown sugar, salt, black pepper, garlic powder, onion powder, and cayenne pepper in a small bowl.

3. Rub the olive oil over the brisket, then evenly coat it with the dry rub.

4. Smoke the brisket for 4-5 hours, or until the internal temperature reaches 93°C, on the smoker grate.

5. Prepare the tangy BBQ sauce while the brisket is smoking. Combine ketchup, apple cider vinegar, Worcestershire sauce, brown sugar, Dijon mustard, smoked paprika, garlic powder, onion powder, salt, and pepper in a small saucepan. Simmer for 15-20 minutes, stirring occasionally, over low heat.

6. Remove the brisket from the smoker after it has reached the desired temperature and allow it to rest for 30 minutes. Then, cut it across the grain.

7. Serve the sliced brisket alongside the tangy BBQ sauce. Enjoy!

NUTRITIONAL INFORMATION: Calories: 455, Protein: 41g, Fat: 27g, Carbohydrates: 7g

SALMON WITH DILL AND LEMON

Prep Time 10 minutes	Cooking Time 1 hour	Servings 2

INGREDIENTS:

- 400 g salmon fillets
- 30 ml olive oil

- 1 tbsp fresh dill, chopped
- Zest of 1 lemon

- Juice of 1/2 lemon
- 1 tsp salt
- 1/2 tsp black pepper

INSTRUCTIONS:

1. Preheat the Ninja Woodfire Grill and Smoker to 80°C on the smoker setting.
2. Season the salmon fillets with salt and black pepper after brushing them with olive oil.
3. Combine the fresh dill, lemon zest, and lemon juice in a small bowl.
4. Place the salmon fillets on the smoker grate and cook for 1-2 hours, depending on their thickness.
5. Brush the salmon fillets with the dill and lemon mixture after 1 hour.
6. Continue to smoke the salmon until it is fully cooked and flakes easily with a fork.
7. Take the smoked salmon out of the smoker and set it aside for a few minutes before serving.
8. If desired, garnish the smoked salmon with additional dill and lemon slices. Enjoy!

NUTRITIONAL INFORMATION: Calories: 284, Protein: 31g, Fat: 17g, Carbohydrates: 2g

PORK RIBS WITH SWEET AND SPICY RUB

Prep Time 10 minutes	Cooking Time 3 hours	Servings 3

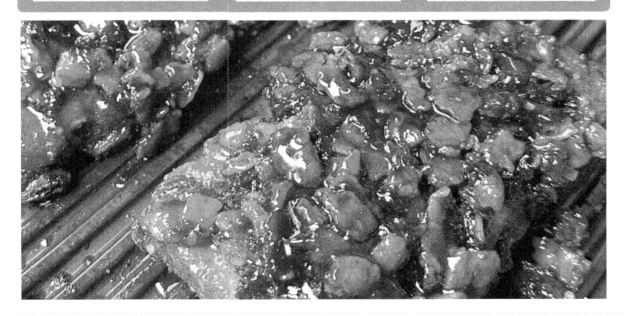

INGREDIENTS:

- 1kg pork ribs
- 40 ml olive oil
- 1 tbsp brown sugar
- 1/2 tbsp paprika
- 1/2 tsp salt
- 1/2 tsp black pepper
- 1/2 tsp garlic powder
- 1/2 tsp onion powder
- 1/2 tsp cayenne pepper
- 200 ml apple juice
- 150 ml BBQ sauce

INSTRUCTIONS:

1. Using the smoker function, preheat the Ninja Woodfire Grill and Smoker to 110°C.

2. To make the dry rub, combine brown sugar, paprika, salt, black pepper, garlic powder, onion powder, and cayenne pepper in a small bowl.

3. Rub the olive oil all over the pork ribs, then coat with the dry rub evenly.

4. Place the pork ribs on the smoker grate for 3 hours to smoke.

5. After 2 hours, baste the ribs every 30 minutes with apple juice to keep them moist.

6. Continue to smoke the ribs until the meat is tender and pulls away from the bone.

7. Brush the ribs with BBQ sauce for a sticky glaze in the last 30 minutes of smoking.

8. Take the smoked pork ribs out of the smoker and set them aside for a few minutes before serving.

9. Serve the smoked pork ribs with extra barbecue sauce on the side. Enjoy!

NUTRITIONAL INFORMATION: Calories: 475, Protein: 35g, Fat: 30g, Carbohydrates: 10g

CHICKEN WINGS WITH MAPLE GLAZE

Prep Time 20 minutes	Cooking Time 1 hours	Servings 2

INGREDIENTS:

- 1/2 kg chicken wings
- 45 ml olive oil
- 1 tsp garlic powder
- 1 tsp smoked paprika
- 1/2 tsp salt
- 1/2 tsp black pepper
- 1/3 tsp cayenne pepper
- 50 ml maple syrup
- 1 tbsp soy sauce
- 1 tbsp apple cider vinegar

INSTRUCTIONS:

1. Preheat the Ninja Woodfire Grill and Smoker to 120°C by using the smoker function.

2. To make the marinade, combine olive oil, garlic powder, smoked paprika, salt, black pepper, and cayenne pepper in a mixing bowl.

3. Toss the chicken wings in the marinade, making sure they are evenly coated. Allow for at least 30 minutes of marinating.

4. Smoke the chicken wings for 1-2 hours, or until the internal temperature reaches 75°C, on the smoker grate.

5. Combine maple syrup, soy sauce, and apple cider vinegar in a small saucepan. To make the glaze, heat the mixture over low heat until it slightly thickens.

6. Brush the chicken wings with the maple glaze every 5 minutes for a sticky coating during the last 15 minutes of smoking.

7. Take the smoked chicken wings out of the smoker and set them aside for a few minutes before serving.

8. Serve the smoked chicken wings with a side of extra maple glaze. Enjoy!

NUTRITIONAL INFORMATION: Calories: 381, Protein: 27g, Fat: 25g, Carbohydrates: 15g

TURKEY BREAST WITH HERB BUTTER

Prep Time 10 minutes	Cooking Time 2 hours	Servings 4

INGREDIENTS:

- 1kg turkey breast
- 40 g unsalted butter, softened
- 1 tbsp fresh herbs (such as thyme, rosemary, sage), chopped

- 1 tsp garlic powder
- 1 tsp salt
- 1/2 tsp black pepper
- 1/2 tsp smoked paprika

INSTRUCTIONS:

1. Preheat the Ninja Woodfire Grill and Smoker to 120°C by using the smoker function.

2. To make the herb butter, combine softened butter, fresh herbs, garlic powder, salt, black pepper, and smoked paprika in a small bowl.

3. Pat the turkey breast-dry with a paper towel before spreading the herb butter all over the surface.

4. Smoke the turkey breast for 2 hours, or until the internal temperature reaches 75°C, on the smoker grate.

5. To keep the turkey breast moist, baste it every 30 minutes with any drippings or melted herb butter.

6. Remove the turkey breast from the smoker once it has reached the desired temperature and allow it to rest for 15-20 minutes before slicing.

7. Serve the smoked turkey breast with your favourite sides. Enjoy!

NUTRITIONAL INFORMATION: Calories: 282, Protein: 41g, Fat: 13g, Carbohydrates: 1g

SAUSAGE AND CHEESE STUFFED JALAPENOS

Prep Time 20 minutes	Cooking Time 1 hour	Servings 4

INGREDIENTS:

- 8 jalapeno peppers
- 100 g cream cheese, softened
- 50 g shredded cheddar cheese
- 50 g smoked sausage, finely chopped
- 1/2 tsp garlic powder
- 1/3 tsp onion powder
- 1/3 tsp smoked paprika
- 1/3 tsp salt
- 1/4 tsp black pepper
- 4 slices bacon, halved

INSTRUCTIONS:

1. Preheat the Ninja Woodfire Grill and Smoker to 120°C with the smoker function.

2. Remove the seeds and membranes from each jalapeno pepper by cutting it in half lengthwise.

3. Mix together cream cheese, shredded cheddar cheese, smoked sausage, garlic powder, onion powder, smoked paprika, salt, and black pepper in a mixing bowl. Combine thoroughly.

4. Spoon the cheese and sausage mixture evenly into each jalapeno half.

5. Wrap a bacon slice around each stuffed jalapeno half and secure with a toothpick.

6. Smoke the stuffed jalapenos for 1 hour, or until the bacon is crispy and the peppers are tender, on the smoker grate.

7. Take the smoked stuffed jalapenos out of the smoker and set them aside for a few minutes to cool before serving.

8. Serve the stuffed jalapenos with smoked sausage and cheese as an appetizer or snack. Enjoy!

NUTRITIONAL INFORMATION: Calories: 182, Protein: 7g, Fat: 13g, Carbohydrates: 5g

PORTOBELLO MUSHROOMS WITH BALSAMIC GLAZE

Prep Time 10 minutes	Cooking Time 1 hour	Servings 2

INGREDIENTS:

- 2 large Portobello mushrooms
- 30 ml olive oil
- 1 cloves garlic, minced
- 1 tbsp balsamic vinegar
- 1/2 tsp dried thyme
- 1/3 tsp salt
- 1/4 tsp black pepper
- Fresh parsley, chopped (for garnish)

INSTRUCTIONS:

1. Preheat the Ninja Woodfire Grill and Smoker to 120°C by using the smoker function.

2. Remove the stems from the Portobello mushrooms and use a spoon to gently scrape out the gills.

3. Whisk together olive oil, minced garlic, balsamic vinegar, dried thyme, salt, and black pepper in a small bowl.

4. Brush the balsamic mixture evenly over both sides of the Portobello mushrooms.

5. Place the mushrooms, gill side up, on the smoker grate and smoke for 1-1.5 hours, or until tender and infused with smoky flavour.

6. Allow the smoked Portobello mushrooms to cool slightly after removing them from the smoker.

7. Before serving, sprinkle the mushrooms with fresh chopped parsley.

8. Smoked Portobello mushrooms can be served as a side dish or as a topping for burgers or salads. Enjoy!

NUTRITIONAL INFORMATION: Calories: 122, Protein: 4g, Fat: 12g, Carbohydrates: 4

BEEF JERKY WITH HOMEMADE MARINADE

Prep Time 15 minutes	Cooking Time 3 hours	Servings 4

INGREDIENTS:

- 300 g beef (e.g., flank steak, sirloin), thinly sliced
- 30 ml soy sauce
- 20 ml Worcestershire sauce
- 30 ml honey
- 10 ml apple cider vinegar
- 1 cloves garlic, minced
- 1 tsp onion powder
- 1/2 tsp smoked paprika
- 1/3 tsp black pepper
- 1/4 tsp salt
- 1/4 tsp cayenne pepper (optional, for heat)

INSTRUCTIONS:

1. To make the marinade, whisk together the soy sauce, Worcestershire sauce, honey, apple cider vinegar, minced garlic, onion powder, smoked paprika, black pepper, salt, and cayenne pepper (if using).

2. Pour the marinade over the thinly sliced beef in a resealable bag or container, making sure all pieces are coated. Marinate for at least 4 hours or overnight in the refrigerator.

3. Preheat the Ninja Woodfire Grill and Smoker to 80°C on the smoker setting.

4. Remove the marinated beef slices and pat them dry with paper towels.

5. Place the beef slices directly on the smoker grate, making sure they don't touch.

6. Smoke the beef slices for 3 hours, or until dry and slightly chewy with a rich smoky flavour.

7. Allow the smoked beef jerky to cool completely before storing it in an airtight container.

8. As a tasty snack, serve the smoked beef jerky. Enjoy!

NUTRITIONAL INFORMATION: Calories: 152, Protein: 23g, Fat: 4g, Carbohydrates: 6g

PULLED PORK SLIDERS WITH COLESLAW

Prep Time 10 minutes	Cooking Time 6-7 hours	Servings 6 sliders

INGREDIENTS:

FOR THE PULLED PORK:

- 1 kg pork shoulder
- 40 ml olive oil
- 1 tbsp brown sugar
- 1 tsp smoked paprika
- 1 tsp garlic powder

- 1 tsp onion powder
- 1 tsp salt
- 1/2 tsp black pepper
- 150 ml apple juice

FOR THE COLESLAW:

- 150 g shredded cabbage
- 60 g grated carrots
- 60 g mayonnaise
- 20 ml apple cider vinegar

- 1 tsp Dijon mustard
- 1 tsp honey
- Salt and pepper to taste

FOR THE SLIDERS:

- Slider buns

INSTRUCTIONS:

1. Preheat the Ninja Woodfire Grill and Smoker to 110°C with the smoker function.

2. To make the dry rub, combine brown sugar, smoked paprika, garlic powder, onion powder, salt, and black pepper in a small bowl.

3. Rub the olive oil all over the pork shoulder before evenly coating it with the dry rub.

4. Smoke the pork shoulder for 6-7 hours, or until it reaches an internal temperature of 90°C and the meat is tender and easily pulls apart.

5. To keep the pork shoulder moist during the last 2 hours of smoking, baste it with apple juice every 30 minutes.

6. Remove the pork shoulder from the smoker and set it aside for 20-30 minutes to rest. Then, using two forks, shred the meat.

7. Combine the shredded cabbage, grated carrots, mayonnaise, apple cider vinegar, Dijon mustard, honey, salt, and pepper in a large mixing bowl. To make the coleslaw, combine all of the ingredients in a mixing bowl.

8. Place a generous amount of smoked pulled pork on each slider bun and assemble the sliders. Serve with a scoop of coleslaw on top.

9. Serve the smoked pulled pork sliders with coleslaw for a tasty and filling meal. Enjoy!

NUTRITIONAL INFORMATION: Calories: 352, Protein: 23g, Fat: 24g, Carbohydrates: 6g

MAC AND CHEESE WITH CRISPY BACON CRUST

Prep Time 20 minutes	Cooking Time 50 minutes	Servings 6-8

INGREDIENTS:

- 600 g elbow macaroni
- 80 g butter
- 80 g all-purpose flour
- 900-1000 ml milk
- 500 g shredded cheddar cheese
- 260 g shredded mozzarella cheese
- 200 g grated Parmesan cheese
- 1 1/2 tsp Dijon mustard
- 1 1/2 tsp smoked paprika
- Salt and pepper to taste
- 8 slices bacon, cooked and crumbled

INSTRUCTIONS:

1. Preheat the Ninja Woodfire Grill and Smoker to 120°C by using the smoker function.

2. Cook the elbow macaroni until al dente according to package directions. Set aside after draining.

3. Melt the butter in a large saucepan over medium heat. Whisk in the flour until smooth.

4. Pour in the milk gradually, whisking constantly, until the mixture thickens and comes to a simmer.

5. Reduce the heat to low and stir in the grated Parmesan cheese, shredded cheddar cheese, and shredded mozzarella cheese. Stir until the cheese has melted and the sauce has thickened.

6. To taste, add the Dijon mustard, smoked paprika, salt, and pepper.

7. Stir in the cooked elbow macaroni until it is evenly coated with the cheese sauce.

8. Place the mac and cheese in a smoker-safe dish or pan.

9. Place the dish or pan on the smoker grate and smoke for 45-50 minutes, or until the mac and cheese has absorbed a smoky flavour and is hot and bubbly.

10. Prepare the crispy bacon crust while the mac and cheese are smoking. Cook the bacon until crispy in a separate pan, then crumble it into small pieces.

11. Remove the smoked mac and cheese from the smoker and evenly sprinkle the crispy bacon crumbles over the top.

12. As a delicious side dish or main course, serve the smoked mac and cheese with crispy bacon crust. Enjoy!

NUTRITIONAL INFORMATION: Calories: 451, Protein: 22g, Fat: 24g, Carbohydrates: 32g

GRILL

RIBEYE STEAK WITH GARLIC BUTTER

Prep Time	Cooking Time	Servings
20 minutes	15-20 minutes	4

INGREDIENTS:

- 4 ribeye steaks (approximately 250 g each)
- 4 cloves garlic, minced
- 50 ml olive oil

- 2 tsp dried thyme
- Salt and pepper to taste
- Fresh parsley, chopped (for garnish)

FOR THE GARLIC BUTTER:

- 60 g unsalted butter, softened
- 4 cloves garlic, minced

- 2 tsp fresh lemon juice
- Salt to taste

INSTRUCTIONS:

1. Preheat the Ninja Woodfire Grill and Smoker to high heat (around 220-230°C) by using the grill function.

2. To make a marinade, combine minced garlic, olive oil, dried thyme, salt, and pepper in a small bowl.

3. Allow the ribeye steaks to sit at room temperature for 15-20 minutes after applying the marinade to both sides.

4. Prepare the garlic butter while the steaks are resting. In a separate mixing bowl, combine softened butter, minced garlic, fresh lemon juice, and salt. Place aside.

5. Cook the marinated ribeye steaks for about 4-5 minutes per side for medium-rare doneness (adjust cooking time based on your preferred level of doneness).

6. Allow the steaks to rest for 5 minutes after they have been removed from the grill to allow the juices to redistribute.

7. Spread a dollop of garlic butter on top of each steak while it rests.

8. For garnish, sprinkle chopped fresh parsley over the steaks.

9. As a main course, serve the grilled ribeye steaks with garlic butter. Enjoy!

NUTRITIONAL INFORMATION: Calories: 405, Protein: 34g, Fat: 34g, Carbohydrates: 1g

LEMON HERB CHICKEN SKEWERS

Prep Time 50 minutes	Cooking Time 15-20 minutes	Servings 4

INGREDIENTS:

- 4 chicken breasts, boneless and skinless, cut into cubes (approximately 300 g)
- Zest and juice of 2 lemon
- 50 ml olive oil
- 3 cloves garlic, minced

- 2 tsp dried oregano
- 2 tsp dried thyme
- Salt and pepper to taste
- Wooden skewers, soaked in water for 50 minutes

INSTRUCTIONS:

1. Preheat the Ninja Woodfire Grill and Smoker to medium-high (around 200-210°C) using the grill function.

2. To make a marinade, combine the lemon zest, lemon juice, olive oil, minced garlic, dried oregano, dried thyme, salt, and pepper in a mixing bowl.

3. Toss the chicken cubes in the marinade until evenly coated. Allow the chicken to marinate for at least 30 minutes in the refrigerator.

4. Thread the soaked wooden skewers with the marinated chicken cubes.

5. Grill the chicken skewers for about 15-20 minutes, turning occasionally, until the chicken is cooked through and has a nice charred exterior.

6. Remove the skewers from the grill and set aside for a few minutes before serving.

7. Grilled lemon herb chicken skewers are a tasty and flavourful appetizer or main course. Enjoy!

NUTRITIONAL INFORMATION: Calories: 305, Protein: 34g, Fat: 20g, Carbohydrates: 4g

SALMON WITH DILL AND LEMON BUTTER SAUCE

Prep Time	Cooking Time	Servings
30 minutes	15-20 minutes	4

INGREDIENTS:

- 4 salmon fillets (approximately 200 g each)
- 50 ml olive oil
- Zest and juice of 1 lemon

- 4 cloves garlic, minced
- 1 1/2 tsp dried dill
- Salt and pepper to taste

FOR THE LEMON BUTTER SAUCE:

- 50 g unsalted butter
- Zest and juice of 1 lemon

- 1 1/2 tbsp chopped fresh dill
- Salt to taste

INSTRUCTIONS:

1. Preheat the Ninja Woodfire Grill and Smoker to medium (around 180-190°C) using the grill function.

2. To make a marinade, combine the olive oil, lemon zest, lemon juice, minced garlic, dried dill, salt, and pepper in a small bowl.

3. Place the salmon fillets in a shallow dish and drizzle with the marinade. Allow the salmon to marinate for about 15-20 minutes.

4. Melt the butter for the lemon butter sauce in a small saucepan over low heat. Combine the lemon zest, lemon juice, fresh dill, and salt in a mixing bowl. Remove from heat and set aside after stirring until well combined.

5. Place the marinated salmon fillets, skin-side down, on a preheated grill and cook for 5-6 minutes.

6. Flip the salmon fillets carefully with a spatula and grill for another 5-6 minutes, or until the salmon is cooked to your desired level of doneness.

7. Remove the grilled salmon from the grill and drizzle with the lemon butter sauce.

8. As a delicious and healthy main course, serve the grilled salmon with dill and lemon butter sauce. Enjoy!

NUTRITIONAL INFORMATION: Calories: 405, Protein: 34g, Fat: 25g, Carbohydrates: 5g

VEGETABLES WITH BALSAMIC GLAZE

Prep Time 20 minutes	Cooking Time 15-20 minutes	Servings 8

INGREDIENTS:

- 4 zucchinis, sliced lengthwise
- 4 bell peppers (assorted colours), seeded and quartered
- 2 red onion, cut into thick slices
- 300 g cherry tomatoes
- 50 ml olive oil
- 4 cloves garlic, minced
- 2 tsp dried oregano
- Salt and pepper to taste
- 100 ml balsamic glaze

INSTRUCTIONS:

1. Preheat the Ninja Woodfire Grill and Smoker to medium-high (around 200-210°C) using the grill function.
2. Combine the zucchini slices, bell pepper quarters, red onion slices, cherry tomatoes, olive oil, minced garlic, dried oregano, salt, and pepper in a large mixing bowl. Toss the vegetables until evenly coated.
3. Cook the vegetables on a preheated grill for 8-10 minutes, turning occasionally, until tender and lightly charred.
4. Take the grilled vegetables off the grill and place them on a serving platter.
5. Drizzle the grilled vegetables with the balsamic glaze.
6. Grilled vegetables with balsamic glaze make a delicious and colourful side dish. Enjoy!

NUTRITIONAL INFORMATION: Calories: 125, Protein: 5g, Fat: 10g, Carbohydrates: 15g

SHRIMP TACOS WITH CHIPOTLE LIME SAUCEE

Prep Time 25 minutes	Cooking Time 10-15 minutes	Servings 6

INGREDIENTS:

FOR THE SHRIMP:
- 500 g shrimp, peeled and deveined
- 50 ml olive oil

- 5 cloves garlic, minced
- 2 tsp chili powder
- 1/2 tsp ground cumin
- Salt and pepper to taste

FOR THE CHIPOTLE LIME SAUCE:
- 200 ml Greek yogurt
- 2 chipotle pepper in adobo sauce, minced
- Zest and juice of 1 lime
- 2 tbsp chopped fresh cilantro
- Salt to taste

FOR SERVING:
- 14-16 small flour tortillas
- Shredded lettuce
- Diced tomatoes
- Sliced avocado
- Lime wedges

INSTRUCTIONS:

1. Preheat the Ninja Woodfire Grill and Smoker to medium (around 180-190°C) using the grill function.
2. Combine the shrimp, olive oil, minced garlic, chili powder, cumin, salt, and pepper in a mixing bowl. Toss the shrimp until evenly coated.
3. Thread the skewers with the marinated shrimp.
4. Cook the shrimp skewers on the preheated grill for about 2-3 minutes per side, or until the shrimp are pink and opaque.
5. Prepare the chipotle lime sauce while the shrimp is grilling. In a small mixing bowl, combine the Greek yogurt, minced chipotle pepper, lime zest, lime juice, cilantro, and salt. Stir until thoroughly combined.
6. Grill the flour tortillas for about 30 seconds per side.
7. Allow the shrimp skewers to cool slightly after removing them from the grill. Take the shrimp off the skewers.
8. Place a spoonful of chipotle lime sauce on each tortilla, then top with shrimp, shredded lettuce, diced tomatoes, and sliced avocado. Squeeze a wedge of lime over each taco.
9. As a flavourful and filling meal, serve the grilled shrimp tacos with chipotle lime sauce. Enjoy!

NUTRITIONAL INFORMATION: Calories: 255, Protein: 20g, Fat: 12g, Carbohydrates: 25g

PORK CHOPS WITH APPLE CIDER GLAZE

Prep Time 20 minutes	Cooking Time 20 minutes	Servings 8

INGREDIENTS:

FOR THE SHRIMP:

- 8 pork chops (approximately 200 g each)
- 60 ml olive oil
- 4 cloves garlic, minced

- 2 tsp dried rosemary
- 2 tsp dried thyme
- Salt and pepper to taste

FOR THE APPLE CIDER GLAZE:

- 200 ml apple cider
- 50 ml soy sauce
- 4 tbsp honey

- 2 tbsp Dijon mustard
- 2 tsp corn-starch mixed with 1 tsp water

INSTRUCTIONS:

1. Preheat the Ninja Woodfire Grill and Smoker to medium-high (around 200-210°C) using the grill function.
2. Combine the olive oil, minced garlic, dried rosemary, dried thyme, salt, and pepper in a small bowl.
3. Brush the mixture evenly over both sides of the pork chops.
4. Combine the apple cider, soy sauce, honey, and Dijon mustard in a small saucepan. Over medium heat, bring the mixture to a boil.
5. In a separate small bowl, make a slurry of corn-starch and water. Stir the slurry into the boiling apple cider mixture until the glaze thickens. Take the pan off the heat.
6. Place the pork chops on a preheated grill and cook for 4-5 minutes per side, or until an internal temperature of 63°C is reached.
7. Allow the apple cider glaze to caramelize on both sides of the pork chops during the last few minutes of grilling.

NUTRITIONAL INFORMATION: Calories: 305, Protein: 30g, Fat: 19g, Carbohydrates: 15g

PORTOBELLO MUSHROOM BURGER WITH AVOCADO MAYO

Prep Time 20 minutes	Cooking Time 20 minutes	Servings 8

INGREDIENTS:

- 8 Portobello mushroom caps
- 60 ml balsamic vinegar
- 60 ml olive oil

- 4 cloves garlic, minced
- 2 tsp dried thyme
- Salt and pepper to taste

FOR THE AVOCADO MAYO:

- 2 ripe avocadoes
- 90 ml mayonnaise

- 2 tbsp lime juice
- Salt and pepper to taste

FOR SERVING:

- 8 burger buns
- Lettuce leaves

- Sliced tomatoes
- Sliced red onions

INSTRUCTIONS:

1. Preheat the Ninja Woodfire Grill and Smoker to medium (around 180-190°C) using the grill function.
2. Clean the Portobello mushroom caps gently with a damp cloth after removing the stems.
3. Whisk together the balsamic vinegar, olive oil, minced garlic, dried thyme, salt, and pepper in a small bowl.
4. Brush the marinade over both sides of the Portobello mushroom caps to coat completely.
5. Cook the mushroom caps for about 4-5 minutes per side on a preheated grill, or until tender and juicy.
6. Prepare the avocado mayo while the mushrooms are grilling. Mash the ripe avocado in a small bowl until smooth. Combine mayonnaise, lime juice, salt, and pepper in a mixing bowl. To combine, combine everything thoroughly.
7. Grill the burger buns for a minute or two on each side.
8. Spread the avocado mayo on the bottom half of each bun and assemble the burgers. Add a grilled Portobello mushroom cap, lettuce leaves, sliced tomatoes, and sliced red onions to the top. Place the bun's top half on top.

9. As a delicious vegetarian option, serve the grilled Portobello mushroom burger with avocado mayo. Enjoy!

NUTRITIONAL INFORMATION: Calories: 285, Protein: 10g, Fat: 18g, Carbohydrates: 29g

PINEAPPLE TERIYAKI CHICKEN SKEWERS

Prep Time 50 minutes	Cooking Time 15-20 minutes	Servings 8

INGREDIENTS:

- 1000 g boneless, skinless chicken breast, cut into bite-sized pieces
- 250 ml teriyaki sauce
- 90 ml pineapple juice
- 60 ml soy sauce
- 4 tbsp honey
- 4 cloves garlic, minced
- 2 tsp grated ginger
- Salt and pepper to taste
- 2 pineapple, peeled and cut into chunks
- 2 red bell pepper, seeded and cut into chunks
- 2 green bell pepper, seeded and cut into chunks
- 2 red onion, cut into chunks
- Wooden skewers, soaked in water for 30 minutes

INSTRUCTIONS:

1. Preheat the Ninja Woodfire Grill and Smoker to medium-high (around 200-210°C) using the grill function.
2. Combine the teriyaki sauce, pineapple juice, soy sauce, honey, minced garlic, grated ginger, salt, and pepper in a mixing bowl. To make the marinade, combine all of the ingredients in a mixing bowl.
3. Pour the marinade over the chicken pieces in a resealable bag. Refrigerate for at least 30 minutes after sealing the bag.
4. Alternately thread the marinated chicken, pineapple chunks, bell peppers, and red onion onto the soaked wooden skewers.
5. Grill the skewers for 8-10 minutes, turning occasionally, until the chicken is cooked through and the vegetables are tender.
6. To enhance the flavour, baste the skewers with any remaining marinade while grilling.
7. Remove the skewers from the grill and set aside for a few minutes before serving.

8. Grilled pineapple teriyaki chicken skewers make a tasty and flavourful meal. Enjoy!

NUTRITIONAL INFORMATION: Calories: 305, Protein: 35g, Fat: 7g, Carbohydrates: 37g

HALLOUMI AND VEGETABLE KEBABS

Prep Time 25 minutes	Cooking Time 15 minutes	Servings 8

INGREDIENTS:

- 500 g halloumi cheese, cut into cubes
- 2 zucchinis, sliced into rounds
- 2 red bell pepper, seeded and cut into chunks
- 2 yellow bell pepper, seeded and cut into chunks
- 2 red onion, cut into chunks
- 50 ml olive oil
- 4 cloves garlic, minced
- 2 tsp dried oregano
- Salt and pepper to taste
- Wooden skewers, soaked in water for 30 minutes

INSTRUCTIONS:

1. Preheat the Ninja Woodfire Grill and Smoker to medium-high (around 200-210°C) using the grill function.

2. Combine the olive oil, minced garlic, dried oregano, salt, and pepper in a mixing bowl. Combine thoroughly.

3. Alternately thread the halloumi cheese, zucchini rounds, bell peppers, and red onion onto the soaked wooden skewers.

4. Brush the olive oil mixture evenly over the skewered vegetables and halloumi.

5. Grill the skewers for 6-8 minutes, turning occasionally, until the halloumi is golden and the vegetables are tender.

6. Allow the grilled halloumi and vegetable kebabs to rest for a few minutes before serving.

7. Serve the kebabs as a tasty and filling vegetarian dish. Enjoy!

NUTRITIONAL INFORMATION: Calories: 285, Protein: 20g, Fat: 15g, Carbohydrates: 17g

PEACHES WITH HONEY AND MASCARPONE

Prep Time 15 minutes	Cooking Time 10-15 minutes	Servings 6

INGREDIENTS:

- 6 ripe peaches, halved and pitted
- 50 ml olive oil
- 3 tbsp honey
- 200 g mascarpone cheese
- Fresh mint leaves for garnish

INSTRUCTIONS:

1. Preheat the Ninja Woodfire Grill and Smoker to medium (around 180-190°C) using the grill function.

2. Brush olive oil on the cut side of each peach half.

3. Cook for 3-4 minutes, or until grill marks appear and the peaches are slightly softened, with the peaches cut side down on a preheated grill.

4. Grill the peaches for another 2-3 minutes on the other side.

5. Take the grilled peaches off the grill and drizzle with honey.

6. Serve with a dollop of mascarpone cheese on top of the grilled peaches.

7. Garnish with fresh mint leaves if desired.

8. Enjoy the flavourful combination of grilled peaches, sweet honey, and creamy mascarpone!

NUTRITIONAL INFORMATION: Calories: 225, Protein: 5g, Fat: 15g, Carbohydrates: 19g

AIR FRYER

CRISPY AIR FRYER CHICKEN WINGS

Prep Time	Cooking Time	Servings
15 minutes	40 minutes	6

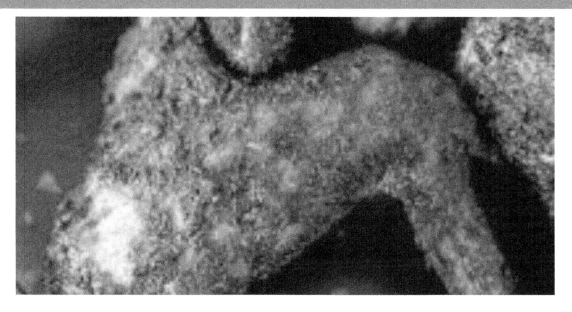

INGREDIENTS:

- 1000g chicken wings
- 3 tbsp olive oil
- 2 tsp garlic powder
- 2 tsp paprika
- 1/2 tsp salt
- 1/3 tsp black pepper
- Optional: buffalo sauce or BBQ sauce for serving

INSTRUCTIONS:

1. Preheat the Ninja Woodfire Grill and Smoker to 200°C with the Air Fryer function.
2. Toss the chicken wings in a large mixing bowl with the olive oil, garlic powder, paprika, salt, and black pepper to coat evenly.
3. Place the chicken wings in the Air Fryer basket in a single layer.
4. Cook the wings in the Air Fryer for 35-40 minutes, flipping halfway through, until they are crispy and golden brown.
5. To add flavour, toss the cooked wings in your favourite buffalo sauce or BBQ sauce.
6. As an appetizer or main course, serve the crispy Air Fryer chicken wings. Enjoy!

NUTRITIONAL INFORMATION: Calories: 355, Protein: 30g, Fat: 20g, Carbohydrates: 2g

FRENCH FRIES WITH GARLIC PARMESAN

Prep Time 20 minutes	Cooking Time 30 minutes	Servings 8

INGREDIENTS:

- 1500g potatoes, cut into fries
- 4 tbsp olive oil
- 4 cloves garlic, minced

- 4 tbsp grated Parmesan cheese
- 2 tsp dried parsley
- Salt and pepper to taste

INSTRUCTIONS:

1. Preheat the Ninja Woodfire Grill and Smoker to 200°C with the Air Fryer function.

2. Toss the cut potatoes with olive oil, minced garlic, grated Parmesan cheese, dried parsley, salt, and pepper in a mixing bowl until evenly coated.

3. Place the seasoned fries in the Air Fryer basket in a single layer.

4. Cook the fries in the Air Fryer for 25-30 minutes, shaking the basket or flipping the fries halfway through, until crispy and golden brown.

5. Remove the fries from the Air Fryer and, if desired, top with additional grated Parmesan cheese.

6. As a side dish or snack, serve the delicious Air Fryer French fries with garlic Parmesan. Enjoy!

NUTRITIONAL INFORMATION: Calories: 225, Protein: 5g, Fat: 10g, Carbohydrates: 30g

MOZZARELLA STICKS WITH MARINARA SAUCE

Prep Time 20 minutes	Cooking Time 20 minutes	Servings 8

INGREDIENTS:

- 500g mozzarella cheese, cut into sticks
- 90g all-purpose flour
- 4 large eggs, beaten
- 200g breadcrumbs
- 2 tsp dried oregano
- 1 tsp garlic powder
- 1 tsp paprika
- 1/3 tsp salt
- Cooking spray
- Marinara sauce, for serving

INSTRUCTIONS:

1. Preheat the Ninja Woodfire Grill and Smoker to 200°C with the Air Fryer function.

2. Set up a breading station with three shallow bowls: flour, beaten eggs, and breadcrumbs seasoned with dried oregano, garlic powder, paprika, and salt.

3. Each mozzarella stick should be dipped in flour, shaking off any excess, then in beaten eggs, and finally in the breadcrumb mixture, pressing lightly to adhere the breadcrumbs.

4. Place the breaded mozzarella sticks in the Air Fryer basket in a single layer.

5. To promote browning, lightly spray the mozzarella sticks with cooking spray.

6. In the Air Fryer, cook the mozzarella sticks for 20 minutes, or until golden and crispy.

7. Serve the mozzarella sticks from the Air Fryer with marinara sauce for dipping. Enjoy!

NUTRITIONAL INFORMATION: Calories: 235, Protein: 15g, Fat: 15g, Carbohydrates: 25g

BBQ CHICKEN DRUMSTICKS

Prep Time 20 minutes	Cooking Time 40 minutes	Servings 6

INGREDIENTS:

- 10 chicken drumsticks
- 3 tbsp olive oil
- 3 tsp paprika
- 2 tsp garlic powder
- 2 tsp onion powder

- 2 tsp dried thyme
- 1 tsp salt
- 1/3 tsp black pepper
- 170ml barbecue sauce

INSTRUCTIONS:

1. Preheat the Ninja Woodfire Grill and Smoker to 200°C with the Air Fryer mode.
2. To create a marinade, put olive oil, paprika, garlic powder, onion powder, dried thyme, salt, and black pepper in a large mixing bowl.
3. Toss the chicken drumsticks in the marinade until fully coated.
4. Place the marinated drumsticks in the Air Fryer basket in a single layer.
5. Cook the drumsticks in the Air Fryer for 30-40 minutes, flipping halfway through, or until cooked through and crispy.
6. Brush the grilled drumsticks with barbecue sauce and continue to heat for another 2-3 minutes to glaze.
7. As a main course, serve the scrumptious Air Fryer BBQ chicken drumsticks. Enjoy!

NUTRITIONAL INFORMATION: Calories: 332, Protein: 28g, Fat: 18g, Carbohydrates: 20g

ZUCCHINI FRIES WITH SRIRACHA AIOLI

Prep Time 20 minutes	Cooking Time 20 minutes	Servings 6

INGREDIENTS:

FOR THE ZUCCHINI FRIES:
- 3 medium zucchinis

- 90g all-purpose flour

- 3 large eggs, beaten
- 200g breadcrumbs
- 1 tsp dried oregano
- 1 tsp garlic powder

- 1 tsp paprika
- 1/3 tsp salt
- Cooking spray

FOR THE SRIRACHA AIOLI:
- 6 tbsp mayonnaise
- 3 tsp Sriracha sauce

- 2 tsp lemon juice
- Salt and pepper to taste

INSTRUCTIONS:

1. Preheat the Ninja Woodfire Grill and Smoker to 200°C with the Air Fryer mode.

2. Slice the zucchini into fry-like sticks.

3. Set up a breading station with three shallow bowls: flour, beaten eggs, and breadcrumbs seasoned with dried oregano, garlic powder, paprika, and salt.

4. Each zucchini stick should be dipped in flour, shaking off any excess, then in beaten eggs, and finally in the breadcrumb mixture, pressing softly to adhere the breadcrumbs.

5. Place the breaded zucchini fries in the Air Fryer basket in a single layer.

6. To encourage browning, lightly coat the zucchini fries with cooking spray.

7. In the Air Fryer, cook the zucchini fries for 12-15 minutes, or until golden and crispy.

8. While the fries are cooking, make the Sriracha aioli in a small bowl by combining mayonnaise, Sriracha sauce, lemon juice, salt, and pepper.

9. Dip the Air Fryer zucchini fries into the Sriracha aioli. Enjoy!

NUTRITIONAL INFORMATION: Calories: 182, Protein: 8g, Fat: 10g, Carbohydrates: 25g

COCONUT SHRIMP WITH SWEET CHILI SAUCE

Prep Time 30 minutes	Cooking Time 20 minutes	Servings 6

INGREDIENTS:

FOR THE COCONUT SHRIMP:
- 350g large shrimp, peeled and deveined
- 90g all-purpose flour

- 3 large eggs, beaten
- 200g breadcrumbs
- 90g desiccated coconut

- 1 tsp paprika
- 1 tsp garlic powder

- 1/3 tsp salt
- Cooking spray

FOR THE SWEET CHILI SAUCE:
- 6 tbsp sweet chili sauce
- 3 tbsp lime juice
- 1 tsp soy sauce

- 1 tsp grated ginger
- 1 tsp minced garlic

INSTRUCTIONS:

1. Preheat the Ninja Woodfire Grill and Smoker to 200°C with the Air Fryer mode.

2. Set up a breading station with three shallow bowls: one with flour, one with beaten eggs, and one with breadcrumbs seasoned with paprika, garlic powder, and salt.

3. Each shrimp should be dipped in the flour, shaking off any excess, then into the beaten eggs, and finally into the breadcrumb and coconut mixture, pressing softly to adhere the coating.

4. Place the breaded shrimp in the Air Fryer basket in a single layer.

5. To encourage browning, lightly coat the shrimp with cooking spray.

6. Cook the shrimp for 8-10 minutes in the Air Fryer, or until brown and crispy.

7. In a separate bowl, combine the sweet chili sauce, lime juice, soy sauce, grated ginger, and minced garlic while the shrimp simmer.

8. Dip the Air Fryer coconut shrimp into the sweet chili sauce. Enjoy!

NUTRITIONAL INFORMATION: Calories: 252, Protein: 17g, Fat: 15g, Carbohydrates: 20g

FALAFEL WITH TZATZIKI SAUCE

Prep Time 25 minutes	Cooking Time 20 minutes	Servings 6

INGREDIENTS:

FOR THE FALAFEL:
- 600g canned chickpeas, drained and rinsed
- 2 small onion, chopped
- 3 cloves garlic, minced

- 3 tbsp chopped fresh parsley
- 1 1/2 tsp ground cumin
- 1 1/2 tsp ground coriander
- 1 tsp salt

- 1/2 tsp black pepper
- 50g breadcrumbs
- Cooking spray

FOR THE TZATZIKI SAUCE:
- 200g Greek yogurt
- 1 cucumber, grated and squeezed to remove excess moisture
- 1 1/2 clove garlic, minced
- 1 1/2 tbsp lemon juice
- 1 1/2 tbsp chopped fresh dill
- Salt and pepper to taste

INSTRUCTIONS:

1. Preheat the Ninja Woodfire Grill and Smoker to 200°C with the Air Fryer mode.
2. Combine chickpeas, onion, garlic, parsley, cumin, coriander, salt, and black pepper in a food processor. Pulse until everything is well blended yet still slightly lumpy.
3. Transfer the mixture to a mixing basin and fold in the breadcrumbs. When pushed, the mixture should hold together.
4. Make tiny patties out of the falafel mixture.
5. Place the falafel patties in the Air Fryer basket in a single layer.
6. Spray the falafel patties lightly with cooking spray.
7. In the Air Fryer, cook the falafel for 12-15 minutes, or until brown and crispy.
8. In a small bowl, combine Greek yogurt, grated cucumber, minced garlic, lemon juice, chopped fresh dill, salt, and pepper to make the tzatziki sauce. Combine thoroughly.
9. Serve the falafel from the Air Fryer with the tzatziki sauce. Enjoy!

NUTRITIONAL INFORMATION: Calories: 212, Protein: 12g, Fat: 8g, Carbohydrates: 30g

VEGETABLE SPRING ROLLS WITH SWEET AND SOUR DIP

Prep Time 15 minutes	Cooking Time 10 minutes	Servings 2

INGREDIENTS:

FOR THE VEGETABLE SPRING ROLLS:
- 4 spring roll wrappers
- 100g mixed vegetables (such as cabbage, carrots, bell peppers), finely shredded
- 30g bean sprouts
- 1 spring onions, thinly sliced
- 1 clove garlic, minced
- 1 tsp grated ginger
- 1 tsp soy sauce
- 1/2 tsp sesame oil

- 1/2 tsp corn-starch mixed with 1 tbsp water

FOR THE SWEET AND SOUR DIP:
- 2 tbsp tomato ketchup
- 1 tbsp rice vinegar
- 1/2 tbsp soy sauce

- Cooking spray

- 1/2 tbsp honey
- 1/3 tsp grated ginger
- 1/3 tsp minced garlic

INSTRUCTIONS:

1. Preheat the Ninja Woodfire Grill and Smoker to 200°C with the Air Fryer mode.
2. Combine the shredded vegetables, bean sprouts, spring onions, garlic, ginger, soy sauce, sesame oil, and corn-starch-water mixture in a mixing bowl. Combine thoroughly.
3. On a clean surface, place a spring roll wrapper. Fill the wrapper with about 2 teaspoons of the veggie mixture, leaving a border on each side.
4. Fold the wrapper's sides over the filling, then roll tightly from the bottom to completely cover it.
5. Wet the top edge of the wrapper and press to seal it. Rep with the rest of the wrappers and filling.
6. Spray the spring rolls lightly with cooking spray and arrange them in the Air Fryer basket in a single layer.
7. In the Air Fryer, cook the spring rolls for 10-12 minutes, or until golden and crispy.
8. In a small bowl, combine tomato ketchup, rice vinegar, soy sauce, honey, grated ginger, and minced garlic to make the sweet and sour dip. Combine thoroughly.
9. Serve the veggie spring rolls from the Air Fryer with the sweet and sour dip. Enjoy!

NUTRITIONAL INFORMATION: Calories: 182, Protein: 7g, Fat: 5g, Carbohydrates: 37g

CRISPY TOFU NUGGETS WITH SPICY PEANUT SAUCE

Prep Time 10 minutes	Cooking Time 10 minutes	Servings 2

INGREDIENTS:

FOR THE CRISPY TOFU NUGGETS:
- 200g firm tofu, drained and pressed
- 1 tbsp corn-starch

- 1/2 tsp garlic powder
- 1/2 tsp paprika

- 1/3 tsp salt
- Cooking spray

FOR THE SPICY PEANUT SAUCE:
- 2 tbsp peanut butter
- 1 tbsp soy sauce
- 1 tbsp lime juice
- 1/2 tbsp maple syrup
- 1/2 tsp Sriracha sauce
- 1/2 clove garlic, minced
- Water (as needed for desired consistency)

INSTRUCTIONS:

1. Preheat the Ninja Woodfire Grill and Smoker to 200°C with the Air Fryer mode.
2. Tofu should be cut into bite-sized bits.
3. Combine corn-starch, garlic powder, paprika, and salt in a shallow basin.
4. To coat the tofu cubes, toss them in the corn-starch mixture.
5. To encourage browning, lightly spray the coated tofu cubes with cooking spray.
6. Place the tofu cubes in the Air Fryer basket in a single layer.
7. In the Air Fryer, cook the tofu for 15-18 minutes, shaking the basket halfway through, until brown and crispy.
8. In a small bowl, combine peanut butter, soy sauce, lime juice, maple syrup, Sriracha sauce, minced garlic, and water (as needed for desired consistency) while the tofu cooks. Combine thoroughly.
9. Serve the crispy tofu nuggets from the Air Fryer with the spicy peanut sauce. Enjoy!

NUTRITIONAL INFORMATION: Calories: 225, Protein: 15g, Fat: 10g, Carbohydrates: 13g

APPLE HAND PIES WITH CARAMEL DRIZZLE

Prep Time 30 minutes	Cooking Time 20 minutes	Servings 8

INGREDIENTS:

FOR THE APPLE FILLING:
- 4 apples, peeled, cored, and finely diced
- 2 tablespoons granulated sugar
- 2 teaspoon lemon juice
- 1 teaspoon ground cinnamon
- 1/3 teaspoon ground nutmeg

FOR THE HAND PIES:
- 4 sheets ready-made puff pastry, thawed
- 2 eggs, beaten (for egg wash)

- Cooking spray

FOR THE CARAMEL DRIZZLE:
- 4 tablespoons caramel sauce

INSTRUCTIONS:

1. Preheat the Ninja Woodfire Grill and Smoker to 180°C with the Air Fryer mode.
2. Combine the diced apples, granulated sugar, lemon juice, cinnamon, and nutmeg in a mixing dish. Mix thoroughly to coat the apples evenly.
3. Roll out the puff pastry sheets and cut them into chosen shapes for the hand pies (circles or squares).
4. Fill each pastry shape with a little quantity of apple filling, leaving a border around the borders.
5. Fold the remaining pastry half over the filling and press the sides together to seal. Crimp the edges with a fork for a decorative touch.
6. To prevent sticking, lightly coat the Air Fryer basket with cooking spray.
7. Place the hand pies in the Air Fryer basket in a single layer, leaving some space between them.
8. Brush the tops of the hand pies lightly with the beaten egg to give them a golden sheen.
9. Air fried the hand pies for 10-12 minutes, or until they are puffed and golden.
10. Warm the caramel sauce in a microwave-safe basin or saucepan while the hand pies bake.
11. Remove the hand pies from the Air Fryer and set aside to cool for a few minutes.
12. Drizzle the hand pies with the heated caramel sauce.
13. Enjoy the warm Air Fryer apple hand pies!

NUTRITIONAL INFORMATION: Calories: 322, Protein: 5g, Fat: 17g, Carbohydrates: 40g

ROAST

CHICKEN WITH LEMON AND HERBS

Prep Time 10 minutes	Cooking Time 30 minutes	Servings 2

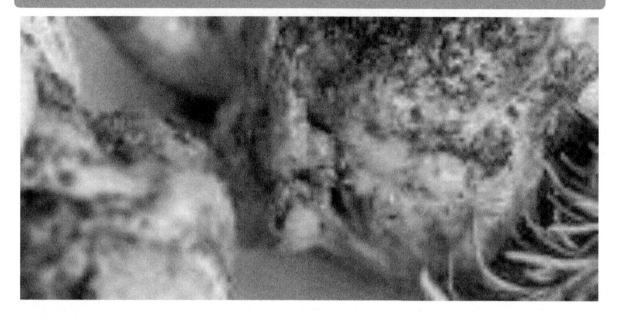

INGREDIENTS:

- 1 whole chicken (about 1 kg)
- 1 lemon
- 3-4 sprigs of fresh rosemary
- 3-4 sprigs of fresh thyme
- 2 cloves of garlic, minced
- 1 tablespoons olive oil
- Salt and pepper to taste

INSTRUCTIONS:

1. Preheat the Ninja Woodfire Grill and Smoker to 180°C by utilizing the "Roast" feature.

2. Rinse the chicken thoroughly, then pat it dry with paper towels.

3. Cut one lemon into slices and place it in the cavity of the chicken, along with some rosemary and thyme sprigs.

4. To produce a paste, combine the minced garlic, olive oil, salt, and pepper in a small bowl.

5. Make sure the chicken is evenly coated with the garlic and herb paste.

6. Place the chicken on the Ninja Woodfire Grill and Smoker on a roasting rack.

7. Cook for 1 hour, or until the internal temperature reaches 75°C and the skin is golden brown and crispy.

8. While the chicken is roasting, squeeze the remaining lemon juice into a small bowl.

9. For added flavour, baste the chicken with lemon juice in the last 10 minutes of cooking.

10. Remove the chicken from the Ninja Woodfire Grill and Smoker and let it rest for 10-15 minutes before carving.

11. Enjoy the roast chicken with lemon and herbs!

NUTRITIONAL INFORMATION: Calories: 252, Protein: 30g, Fat: 17g, Carbohydrates: 4g

HERB-CRUSTED ROAST BEEF WITH RED WINE JUS

Prep Time 10 minutes	Cooking Time 15 minutes	Servings 3

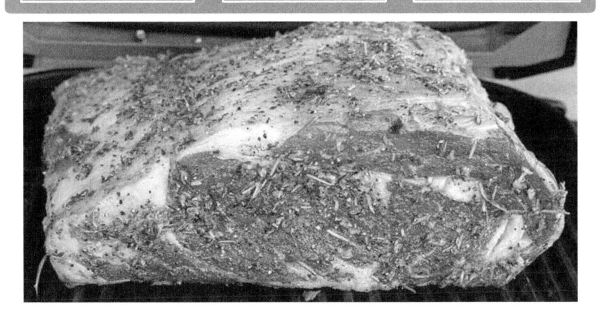

INGREDIENTS:

- 1 kg beef roast (e.g., ribeye, sirloin)
- 2 tablespoons Dijon mustard
- 2 tablespoons fresh thyme leaves, chopped
- 2 tablespoons fresh rosemary leaves, chopped
- 2 tablespoons fresh parsley leaves, chopped
- 2 cloves of garlic, minced
- 1 tablespoons olive oil
- Salt and pepper to taste

FOR THE RED WINE JUS:
- 100 ml red wine
- 100 ml beef broth
- 2 tablespoons butter

INSTRUCTIONS:

1. Preheat the Ninja Woodfire Grill and Smoker to 180°C by utilizing the "Roast" feature.

2. To make a paste, combine the Dijon mustard, chopped thyme, rosemary, parsley, minced garlic, olive oil, salt, and pepper in a small bowl.

3. Rub the herb paste all over the meat roast to coat it evenly.

4. Place the roast on the Ninja Woodfire Grill and Smoker on a roasting rack.

5. Roast the beef for around 20 minutes per 500 grams for medium-rare doneness, or alter the cooking time to your preference.

6. Prepare the red wine jus while the steak is cooking. Combine the red wine and beef broth in a saucepan. Cook, stirring occasionally, until the liquid has reduced by half.

7. Remove the roast beef from the Ninja Woodfire Grill and Smoker and let it rest for 15-20 minutes before slicing.

8. While the meat is resting, make a smooth jus by whisking the butter into the red wine reduction.

9. Serve the roast meat sliced with the red wine jus.

NUTRITIONAL INFORMATION: Calories: 355, Protein: 38g, Fat: 20g, Carbohydrates: 4g

GARLIC AND ROSEMARY ROASTED LAMB LEG

Prep Time 20 minutes	Cooking Time 20 minutes	Servings 10

INGREDIENTS:

- 1.5 kg lamb leg
- 5 cloves of garlic, minced
- 2 tablespoons fresh rosemary leaves, chopped
- 2 tablespoons olive oil
- Salt and pepper to taste

INSTRUCTIONS:

1. Preheat the Ninja Woodfire Grill and Smoker to 180°C using the "Roast" function.

2. In a small bowl, mix together the minced garlic, chopped rosemary, olive oil, salt, and pepper to create a paste.

3. Rub the garlic and rosemary paste all over the lamb leg, ensuring it is evenly coated.

4. Place the lamb leg on a roasting rack and put it in the Ninja Woodfire Grill and Smoker.

5. Roast the lamb leg for about 25 minutes per 500 grams for medium-rare doneness or adjust the cooking time according to your preference.

6. Once the lamb leg is cooked to your liking, remove it from the Ninja Woodfire Grill and Smoker and let it rest for 15-20 minutes before carving.

7. Slice the lamb leg and serve it with your favourite side dishes.

NUTRITIONAL INFORMATION: Calories: 405, Protein: 50g, Fat: 20g, Carbohydrates: 2g

PORK TENDERLOIN WITH APPLE AND SAGE STUFFING

Prep Time 10 minutes	Cooking Time 15 minutes	Servings 2

INGREDIENTS:

- 400g pork tenderloin
- 1 tablespoons olive oil

- Salt and pepper to taste

FOR THE APPLE AND SAGE STUFFING:
- 1/2 tablespoon butter
- 1/2 small onion, finely chopped
- 1 clove of garlic, minced
- 1 apple, peeled, cored, and diced

- 1/2 teaspoon dried sage
- 1/2 teaspoon dried thyme
- 30 g breadcrumbs
- Salt and pepper to taste

INSTRUCTIONS:

1. Preheat the Ninja Woodfire Grill and Smoker to 180°C by utilizing the "Roast" feature.

2. Melt the butter in a large skillet over medium heat. Cook until the onion and garlic are softened, about 5 minutes.

3. To the skillet, add the chopped apples, dried sage, dry thyme, salt, and pepper. Cook for a few minutes longer, or until the apples are soft.

4. Remove from the heat and toss in the breadcrumbs until thoroughly mixed.

5. Butterfly the tenderloin by cutting it lengthwise and folding it open like a book. Pound the meat until it is a uniform thickness.

6. Fill the pork tenderloin with the apple and sage filling, leaving a border around the edges.

7. Roll the pork tenderloin up tightly and tie with kitchen twine.

8. Rub the rolled pork tenderloin with the olive oil, salt, and pepper.

9. Put the pork tenderloin on a roasting rack in the Ninja Woodfire Grill and Smoker.

10. Roast the pork tenderloin for 20-25 minutes, or until it reaches an internal temperature of 63°C.

11. When the pork tenderloin is done, remove it from the Ninja Woodfire Grill & Smoker and set it aside for 5-10 minutes before slicing.

12. Serve the pork tenderloin with your favourite side dishes.

NUTRITIONAL INFORMATION: Calories: 305, Protein: 34g, Fat: 11g, Carbohydrates: 14g

TURKEY WITH CRANBERRY GLAZE

Prep Time 15 minutes	Cooking Time 3 hours	Servings 6-7

INGREDIENTS:

- 2 kg turkey
- 50 g unsalted butter, softened
- Salt and pepper to taste

FOR THE CRANBERRY GLAZE:
- 150 g cranberry sauce
- 2 tablespoons honey
- 1 tablespoon balsamic vinegar
- 1 teaspoon Dijon mustard

INSTRUCTIONS:

1. Preheat the Ninja Woodfire Grill and Smoker to 180°C by utilizing the "Roast" feature.

2. Thoroughly rinse the turkey and pat it dry with paper towels.

3. Season the turkey on all sides with salt and pepper.

4. In a roasting pan, place the turkey on a roasting rack.

5. Rub the softened butter all over the turkey, making sure to evenly coat the skin.

6. To make the glaze, whisk together the cranberry sauce, honey, balsamic vinegar, and Dijon mustard in a small basin.

7. Brush the cranberry glaze generously over the turkey, saving some for basting during cooking.

8. Cook the turkey in the Ninja Woodfire Grill and Smoker for around 20 minutes per kilogram, or until the internal temperature of the thickest section of the turkey reaches 75°C.

9. Every 30 minutes, baste the bird with the reserved glaze.

10. When the turkey is done, remove it from the Ninja Woodfire Grill and Smoker and set it aside for 20-30 minutes before cutting.

11. Carve the turkey and serve it alongside your favourite sides.

NUTRITIONAL INFORMATION: Calories: 452, Protein: 51g, Fat: 26g, Carbohydrates: 7g

VEGETABLES WITH BALSAMIC REDUCTION

Prep Time 20 minutes	Cooking Time 40 minutes	Servings 6

INGREDIENTS:

- 1000 g mixed vegetables (e.g., carrots, parsnips, potatoes, Brussels sprouts), cut into bite-sized pieces
- 4 tablespoons olive oil
- Salt and pepper to taste
- 3 tablespoons balsamic vinegar
- 2 tablespoon honey

INSTRUCTIONS:

1. Preheat the Ninja Woodfire Grill and Smoker to 200°C on the "Roast" setting.

2. Toss the mixed vegetables with olive oil, salt, and pepper in a large mixing bowl until completely covered.

3. On a roasting pan, equally distribute the vegetables.

4. Place the roasting pan in the Ninja Woodfire Grill and Smoker and roast for 25-30 minutes, or until the veggies are tender and slightly browned.

5. Meanwhile, combine the balsamic vinegar and honey in a small saucepan. Bring the mixture to a simmer over medium heat and cook until it thickens and reduces by half.

6. After the roasted vegetables have been removed from the Ninja Woodfire Grill and Smoker, sprinkle them with the balsamic reduction.

7. Gently toss the vegetables in the reduction to coat evenly.

8. Roasted vegetables make an excellent side dish.

NUTRITIONAL INFORMATION: Calories: 205, Protein: 5g, Fat: 7g, Carbohydrates: 31g

DUCK WITH ORANGE AND THYME

Prep Time 10 minutes	Cooking Time 2 hours	Servings 4

INGREDIENTS:

- 2 kg whole duck
- 2 oranges, zest and juice
- 3 sprigs of fresh thyme
- Salt and pepper to taste

INSTRUCTIONS:

1. Preheat the Ninja Woodfire Grill and Smoker to 180°C by using the "Roast" function.

2. Rinse the duck under cold running water and pat dry with paper towels.

3. Season the duck on all sides with salt, pepper, and orange zest.

4. Insert the remaining orange quarters and fresh thyme sprigs into the duck cavity.

5. To keep the stuffing in place, tie the legs together with kitchen twine.

6. In a roasting pan, place the duck on a roasting rack.

7. Roast the duck for 2.5 to 3 hours in the Ninja Woodfire Grill and Smoker, or until the skin is crispy and the internal temperature reaches 75°C.

8. In a small saucepan, combine the juice of one orange and any remaining zest with a pinch of salt and pepper while the duck roasts. Simmer on low heat until the sauce thickens into a glaze.

9. During cooking, baste the duck with the orange glaze every 30 minutes.

10. When the duck is done, remove it from the Ninja Woodfire Grill and Smoker and set it aside for 15-20 minutes before carving.

11. Serve the duck with the remaining orange glaze as a sauce.

NUTRITIONAL INFORMATION: Calories: 405, Protein: 31g, Fat: 32g, Carbohydrates: 3g

SALMON WITH DILL AND LEMON BUTTER SAUCE

Prep Time 10 minutes	Cooking Time 10 minutes	Servings 2

INGREDIENTS:

- 2 salmon fillets
- Salt and pepper to taste
- 1 tablespoon melted butter
- 1 tablespoons lemon juice
- 1 tablespoon chopped fresh dill
- Lemon slices for garnish

INSTRUCTIONS:

1. Preheat the Ninja Woodfire Grill and Smoker to 200°C on the "Roast" setting.

2. Season both sides of the salmon fillets with salt and pepper.

3. Place the salmon fillets on a baking sheet that has been greased.

4. Combine the melted butter, lemon juice, and dill in a small bowl.

5. Drizzle the butter mixture evenly over the salmon fillets.

6. In the Ninja Woodfire Grill and Smoker, place the baking sheet with the salmon.

7. Cook for 12-15 minutes, or until the salmon flakes easily with a fork and reaches an internal temperature of 60°C.

8. Allow the salmon to rest for a few minutes after removing it from the Ninja Woodfire Grill and Smoker.

9. Serve the roasted salmon with lemon slices and cooking juices drizzled on top.

NUTRITIONAL INFORMATION: Calories: 305, Protein: 31g, Fat: 24g, Carbohydrates: 3g

RACK OF LAMB WITH MINT PESTO

Prep Time 15 minutes	Cooking Time 35 minutes	Servings 4

INGREDIENTS:

- 2 rack of lamb (about 800 grams)
- Salt and pepper to taste
- 3 tablespoons olive oil

- 3 cloves garlic, minced
- 3 tablespoons fresh rosemary, chopped

FOR THE MINT PESTO:

- 50 grams fresh mint leaves
- 50 grams fresh parsley leaves
- 50 grams pine nuts
- 3 cloves garlic

- 100 ml extra virgin olive oil
- Juice of 1/2 lemon
- Salt and pepper to taste

INSTRUCTIONS:

1. Preheat the Ninja Woodfire Grill and Smoker to 200°C on the "Roast" setting.

2. Season the rack of lamb with salt and pepper to taste.

3. Combine the olive oil, minced garlic, and rosemary in a small bowl.

4. Apply the mixture to the rack of lamb.

5. In a roasting pan, place the rack of lamb on a roasting rack.

6. Roast the lamb for 25-30 minutes in the Ninja Woodfire Grill and Smoker for medium-rare doneness (internal temperature of 55-60°C).

7. Prepare the mint pesto while the lamb is roasting. Combine the mint leaves, parsley leaves, pine nuts, garlic, olive oil, lemon juice, salt, and pepper in a food processor. Blend until well combined.

8. When the lamb is cooked to your liking, remove it from the Ninja Woodfire Grill and Smoker and set it aside for 10 minutes before carving.

9. Serve the rack of lamb cut into individual chops with the mint pesto.

NUTRITIONAL INFORMATION: Calories: 402, Protein: 33g, Fat: 27g, Carbohydrates: 3g

BUTTERNUT SQUASH WITH MAPLE GLAZE

Prep Time 15 minutes	Cooking Time 40 minutes	Servings 6

INGREDIENTS:

- 2 medium butternut squash, peeled, seeded, and cut into cubes
- 3 tablespoons olive oil
- 3 tablespoons maple syrup
- 2 teaspoon ground cinnamon
- Salt and pepper to taste
- Fresh parsley, chopped (for garnish)

INSTRUCTIONS:

1. Preheat the Ninja Woodfire Grill and Smoker to 200°C on the "Roast" setting.

2. Combine the cubed butternut squash, olive oil, maple syrup, ground cinnamon, salt, and pepper in a large mixing bowl. Toss to evenly coat the squash.

3. Arrange the butternut squash cubes on a baking sheet or roasting pan.

4. Roast the butternut squash for 25-30 minutes, or until tender and caramelized, in the Ninja Woodfire Grill and Smoker, stirring once halfway through.

5. Transfer the roasted butternut squash to a serving dish from the Ninja Woodfire Grill and Smoker.

6. Before serving, garnish with fresh chopped parsley.

NUTRITIONAL INFORMATION: Calories: 155, Protein: 3g, Fat: 8g, Carbohydrates: 25g

BAKE

CLASSIC CHOCOLATE CHIP COOKIES

Prep Time 10 minutes	Cooking Time 10 minutes	Servings About 12 cookies

INGREDIENTS:

- 110g unsalted butter, softened
- 100g granulated sugar
- 100g light brown sugar
- 1 large eggs
- 3ml vanilla extract
- 180g all-purpose flour
- 3ml baking soda
- 3ml salt
- 150g chocolate chips

INSTRUCTIONS:

1. Preheat the Ninja Woodfire Grill and Smoker to 180 degrees Celsius.

2. Cream together the softened butter, granulated sugar, and brown sugar in a large mixing bowl until light and fluffy.

3. One at a time, beat in the eggs, followed by the vanilla extract.

4. Whisk together the flour, baking soda, and salt in a separate bowl. Add the dry ingredients to the butter mixture gradually, mixing until just combined.

5. Incorporate the chocolate chips.

6. Place rounded tablespoons of dough on a lined baking sheet, about 5cm apart.

7. Bake for 12-15 minutes, or until golden brown around the edges, on a preheated grill.

8. Allow the cookies to cool for a few minutes on the baking sheet before transferring to a wire rack to cool completely.

9. Serve and have fun!

NUTRITIONAL INFORMATION: Calories: 155 kcal, Fat: 7g, Carbohydrates: 17g, Protein: 3g

HOMEMADE PIZZA WITH FRESH TOMATO SAUCE

Prep Time 15 minutes	Cooking Time 10 minutes	Servings 1 large pizza

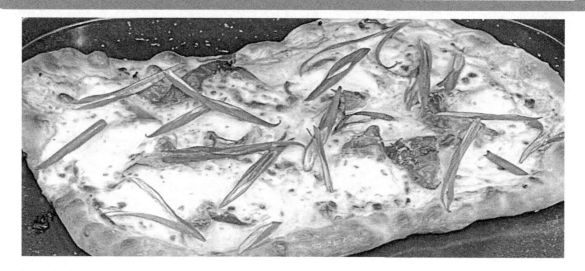

INGREDIENTS:

FOR THE DOUGH:

- 250g strong bread flour
- 5g instant yeast
- 3ml salt
- 170ml warm water

FOR THE TOMATO SAUCE:
- 200g canned tomatoes, crushed
- 15ml tomato paste
- 8ml olive oil
- 1 cloves garlic, minced
- 3ml dried oregano
- 3ml sugar
- Salt and pepper to taste

FOR THE TOPPINGS:
- Mozzarella cheese, grated
- Your choice of toppings (e.g., sliced tomatoes, sliced mushrooms, sliced peppers, olives, etc.)

INSTRUCTIONS:

1. Preheat the Ninja Woodfire Grill and Smoker to 220 degrees Celsius.

2. Combine the flour, yeast, and salt in a large mixing bowl. Mix in the warm water gradually until a dough form.

3. Knead the dough for 5 minutes on a floured surface, or until smooth and elastic. Allow the dough to rest for 10 minutes after dividing it into two equal parts.

4. Meanwhile, heat the olive oil in a saucepan over medium heat to make the tomato sauce. Cook for 1-2 minutes, or until the garlic is fragrant. Combine the crushed tomatoes, tomato paste, dried oregano, sugar, salt, and pepper in a mixing bowl. Simmer for 10-15 minutes, or until the sauce has thickened.

5. Roll each dough portion into a thin circle and place it on pizza pans or baking sheets.

6. Cover the dough with the tomato sauce, leaving a small border around the edges. Top with your preferred toppings and grated mozzarella cheese.

7. Bake for 15-20 minutes, or until the crust is golden brown and the cheese is bubbly and slightly browned, on a preheated grill.

8. Remove from the grill, slice, and serve while still hot.

NUTRITIONAL INFORMATION: Calories: 151 kcal (per slice), Fat: 12g, Carbohydrates: 30g, Protein: 10g

CHEESY GARLIC BREAD ROLLS

Prep Time 15 minutes	Cooking Time 10 minutes	Servings 6 rolls

INGREDIENTS:

- 250g bread flour
- 4g instant yeast
- 3ml salt
- 15ml olive oil
- 150ml warm water

- 4 cloves garlic, minced
- 40g unsalted butter, melted
- 15g Parmesan cheese, grated
- 150g mozzarella cheese, shredded
- Fresh parsley, chopped (for garnish)

INSTRUCTIONS:

1. Preheat the Ninja Woodfire Grill and Smoker to 200 degrees Celsius.

2. Combine the bread flour, yeast, and salt in a large mixing bowl. Combine the olive oil and warm water in a mixing bowl. Blend until a dough form.

3. Turn the dough out onto a floured surface and knead for 5-7 minutes, or until smooth and elastic. Return the dough to the bowl, cover with a damp cloth, and set aside for 1 hour, or until doubled in size.

4. Punch the dough down and divide it into 12 equal parts. Make a ball out of each portion.

5. Combine the minced garlic and melted butter in a small bowl.

6. Dip each dough ball into the garlic butter mixture, coating completely.

7. Place the coated dough balls, leaving some space between them, in a greased baking dish. Sprinkle with grated Parmesan and shredded mozzarella cheese.

8. Bake for 15-20 minutes, or until the rolls are golden brown and the cheese is melted and bubbly, on a preheated grill.

9. Remove from the grill and serve warm, garnished with fresh parsley.

NUTRITIONAL INFORMATION: Calories: 100 kcal (per roll), Fat: 5g, Carbohydrates: 15g, Protein: 3g

BLUEBERRY STREUSEL MUFFINS

Prep Time 10 minutes	Cooking Time 15 minutes	Servings 6 muffins

INGREDIENTS:

FOR THE STREUSEL TOPPING:
- 30g plain flour
- 30g granulated sugar

- 15g unsalted butter, melted

FOR THE MUFFINS:
- 150g plain flour
- 5g baking powder
- 1g salt
- 50g granulated sugar
- 60ml milk
- 40ml vegetable oil
- 1 large eggs
- 3ml vanilla extract
- 100g fresh blueberries

INSTRUCTIONS:

1. Preheat the Ninja Woodfire Grill and Smoker to 180 degrees Celsius.

2. In a small mixing bowl, combine the streusel topping ingredients: flour, sugar, and melted butter. Place aside.

3. Whisk together the flour, baking powder, salt, and sugar in a large mixing bowl.

4. Combine the milk, vegetable oil, eggs, and vanilla extract in a separate bowl. Whisk until well combined.

5. Stir the wet ingredients into the dry ingredients until they are just combined. Avoid overmixing.

6. Fold in the fresh blueberries gently.

7. Prepare a muffin pan with paper liners. Divide the batter evenly among the muffin cups, about two-thirds full.

8. Spread the streusel topping on top of each muffin.

9. Bake for 20-25 minutes, or until a toothpick inserted into the centre of a muffin comes out clean.

10. Remove the muffins from the oven and set aside for a few minutes to cool. Allow to cool completely on a wire rack before serving.

NUTRITIONAL INFORMATION: Calories: 110 kcal (per muffin), Fat: 6g, Carbohydrates: 15g, Protein: 2g

CINNAMON SWIRL BANANA BREAD

Prep Time	Cooking Time	Servings
20 minutes	1 hour 30 minutes	2 loafs

INGREDIENTS:

- 250g plain flour
- 5g baking powder
- 2g baking soda
- 3g ground cinnamon

- 2g salt
- 100g unsalted butter, softened
- 150g granulated sugar
- 2 large eggs
- 5ml vanilla extract
- 3 ripe bananas, mashed
- 60ml milk

FOR THE CINNAMON SWIRL:

- 30g granulated sugar
- 5g ground cinnamon

INSTRUCTIONS:

1. Preheat the Ninja Woodfire Grill and Smoker to 180 degrees Celsius.
2. In a medium mixing bowl, combine the flour, baking powder, baking soda, cinnamon, and salt.
3. Cream together the softened butter and granulated sugar in a separate large mixing bowl until light and fluffy.
4. One at a time, beat in the eggs, followed by the vanilla extract.
5. Mix in the mashed bananas with the butter mixture until well combined.
6. Alternately add the dry ingredients and milk to the wet ingredients. Mix until everything is just combined.
7. For the cinnamon swirl, combine the granulated sugar and ground cinnamon in a small bowl.
8. Half of the banana bread batter should be placed in a greased loaf pan. Half of the cinnamon swirl mixture should be sprinkled over the batter. Sprinkle the remaining cinnamon swirl mixture on top of the remaining batter.
9. Swirl the cinnamon mixture into the batter with a knife to create a marbled effect.
10. Bake for 50-60 minutes, or until a toothpick inserted into the centre of the bread comes out clean.
11. Remove the bread from the grill and let it cool in the pan for 10 minutes. Cool completely on a wire rack before slicing and serving.

NUTRITIONAL INFORMATION: Calories: 255 kcal (per slice), Fat: 12g, Carbohydrates: 33g, Protein: 5g

SAVORY SPINACH AND FETA GALETTE

Prep Time 20 minutes	Cooking Time 25 minutes	Servings 4

INGREDIENTS:

FOR THE PASTRY:

- 180g plain flour
- 5g salt
- 100g unsalted butter, cold and cubed
- 60ml ice water

FOR THE FILLING:

- 150g fresh spinach
- 60g feta cheese, crumbled
- 40g cherry tomatoes, halved
- 1 small red onion, thinly sliced
- 1 clove garlic, minced
- 15ml olive oil
- Salt and pepper to taste
- 1 egg, beaten (for egg wash)

INSTRUCTIONS:

1. Preheat the Ninja Woodfire Grill and Smoker to 200 degrees Celsius.

2. Whisk together the flour and salt for the pastry in a large mixing bowl. Rub in the cold cubed butter with your fingertips until the mixture resembles coarse breadcrumbs.

3. Add the ice water a little at a time, mixing until the dough comes together. Form the dough into a ball, flatten it into a disc, wrap it in plastic wrap, and place it in the refrigerator for 15 minutes.

4. Meanwhile, heat the olive oil in a saucepan over medium heat. Cook until the minced garlic and sliced red onion are softened. Sauté the fresh spinach until wilted. Season to taste with salt and pepper. Remove from the heat and leave to cool.

5. Roll out the chilled pastry into a circle about 30cm in diameter on a lightly floured surface. Place the rolled pastry on a baking sheet that has been lined with parchment paper.

6. Spread the sautéed spinach mixture over the pastry, leaving a 5cm border. Sprinkle feta cheese crumbles over the spinach. On top, arrange the cherry tomato halves.

7. Fold the pastry edges over the filling, pleating as needed. Brush the pastry's edges with beaten egg wash.

8. Bake for 25-30 minutes, or until the pastry is golden brown and crispy, in a preheated grill.

9. Remove from the grill and set aside for a few minutes to cool before serving. Serve warm, sliced.

NUTRITIONAL INFORMATION: Calories: 301 kcal, Fat: 19g, Carbohydrates: 23g, Protein: 12g

GARLIC PARMESAN CHICKEN PARMESAN

Prep Time 10 minutes	Cooking Time 15 minutes	Servings 2

INGREDIENTS:

- 2 chicken breasts
- 1 cloves garlic, minced
- 30g grated Parmesan cheese
- 30g breadcrumbs
- 10g dried parsley

- 3g dried oregano
- 3g dried basil
- Salt and pepper to taste
- 20ml olive oil

INSTRUCTIONS:

1. Preheat the Ninja Woodfire Grill and Smoker to 200 degrees Celsius.

2. Mix together the minced garlic, grated Parmesan cheese, breadcrumbs, dried parsley, dried oregano, dried basil, salt, and pepper in a mixing bowl.

3. Brush each chicken breast with olive oil and evenly coat with the garlic Parmesan mixture.

4. Line a baking sheet with parchment paper and place the coated chicken breasts on it.

5. Bake for 20-25 minutes, or until the chicken is cooked through and the coating is golden brown and crispy, on a preheated grill.

6. Remove the chicken from the grill and set aside for a few minutes before serving. Serve with your preferred side dishes.

NUTRITIONAL INFORMATION: Calories: 401 kcal, Fat: 22g, Carbohydrates: 14g, Protein: 43g

APPLE CINNAMON CRUMBLE PIE

Prep Time 15 minutes	Cooking Time 40 minutes	Servings 4

INGREDIENTS:

FOR THE CRUST:
- 200g plain flour
- 3g salt
- 100g unsalted butter, cold and cubed
- 30ml ice water

FOR THE FILLING:
- 600g apples, peeled, cored, and sliced
- 30g granulated sugar
- 10g plain flour
- 3g ground cinnamon
- 5g lemon juice

FOR THE CRUMBLE TOPPING:
- 55g plain flour
- 55g rolled oats
- 55g brown sugar
- 55g unsalted butter, cold and cubed

INSTRUCTIONS:

1. Preheat the Ninja Woodfire Grill and Smoker to 180 degrees Celsius.

2. Whisk together the flour and salt for the crust in a large mixing bowl. Rub in the cold cubed butter with your fingertips until the mixture resembles coarse breadcrumbs.

3. Add the ice water a little at a time, mixing until the dough comes together. Form the dough into a ball, flatten it into a disc, wrap it in plastic wrap, and place it in the refrigerator for 15 minutes.

4. Combine the sliced apples, granulated sugar, flour, ground cinnamon, and lemon juice in a separate bowl. Toss the apples until they are evenly coated.

5. In a separate bowl, combine the flour, rolled oats, brown sugar, and cold cubed butter to make the crumble topping. Using your fingertips, combine the ingredients until they resemble coarse crumbs.

6. Roll out the chilled pastry into a circle large enough to fit into a pie dish on a lightly floured surface. Place the rolled pastry in the pie dish, gently pressing it into the bottom and sides.

7. Fill the pastry-lined dish with the apple filling. Evenly distribute the crumble topping over the apples.

8. Place the pie dish on a baking sheet and bake for 40-45 minutes, or until the crust is golden brown and the filling is bubbly, in a preheated grill.

9. Remove from the grill and set aside for a few minutes to cool before serving. If desired, serve warm with a scoop of vanilla ice cream.

NUTRITIONAL INFORMATION: Calories: 355 kcal (per serving), Fat: 13g, Carbohydrates: 52g, Protein: 3g

CHEDDAR AND BACON STUFFED PRETZELS

Prep Time 60 minutes	Cooking Time 10 minutes	Servings 4

INGREDIENTS:

FOR THE PRETZEL DOUGH:
- 150ml warm water
- 1 /2 tsp sugar
- 4g instant yeast
- 250g plain flour
- 5g salt
- 20g unsalted butter, melted

FOR THE FILLING:
- 80g cheddar cheese, cut into small cubes
- 4 slices bacon, cooked and crumbled

FOR THE TOPPING:
- 20g unsalted butter, melted
- Coarse salt, for sprinkling

INSTRUCTIONS:

1. Preheat the Ninja Woodfire Grill and Smoker to 200 degrees Celsius.

2. Warm water, sugar, and yeast should all be combined in a small bowl. Allow it to sit for 5 minutes, or until foamy.

3. Whisk together the flour and salt in a large mixing bowl. To the flour, add the melted butter and yeast mixture. Mix the dough until it comes together.

4. Knead the dough for 5-7 minutes on a lightly floured surface, until smooth and elastic.

5. Place the dough in a greased mixing bowl, cover with a clean kitchen towel, and set aside for 1 hour, or until doubled in size.

6. Punch the dough down to release the air. Cut the dough into 8 equal pieces.

7. Make a rope out of each portion and flatten it with your hands. In the centre of each piece of dough, place a few cubes of cheddar cheese and some crumbled bacon. Fold the dough over the filling and seal the edges.

8. Make each stuffed dough pretzel shape.

9. Line a baking sheet with parchment paper and place the pretzels on it. Brush the pretzels with melted butter and season with salt.

10. Bake for 12-15 minutes, or until the pretzels are golden brown, in a preheated grill.

11. Remove from the grill and set aside for a few minutes to cool before serving. Warm pretzels are best.

NUTRITIONAL INFORMATION: Calories: 401 kcal (per pretzel), Fat: 19g, Carbohydrates: 42g, Protein: 14g

RASPBERRY WHITE CHOCOLATE SCONES

Prep Time 10 minutes	Cooking Time 10-15 minutes	Servings 4

INGREDIENTS:

- 150g self-rising flour
- 30g caster sugar
- 1/3 tsp baking powder
- 35g unsalted butter, cold and cubed
- 80ml milk
- 1/2 tsp vanilla extract
- 60g white chocolate, chopped
- 50g fresh raspberries

INSTRUCTIONS:

1. Preheat the Ninja Woodfire Grill and Smoker to 200 degrees Celsius.

2. Whisk together the self-rising flour, caster sugar, and baking powder in a large mixing bowl.

3. To the flour mixture, add the cold cubed butter. Rub the butter into the flour with your fingertips until it resembles breadcrumbs.

4. Whisk together the milk and vanilla extract in a separate bowl. Add the milk mixture to the dry ingredients gradually, stirring with a fork until the dough comes together.

5. To the dough, add the chopped white chocolate and fresh raspberries. Gently knead the dough a few times to evenly distribute the add-ins.

6. Pat the dough into a 2cm thick circle on a lightly floured surface. Cut scones from the dough with a round cookie cutter.

7. Line a baking sheet with parchment paper and place the scones on it. Brush the scones' tops with a little milk.

8. Bake for 15-18 minutes, or until the scones are golden brown and cooked through, on a preheated grill.

9. Remove the scones from the grill and set aside for a few minutes before serving. Warm or at room temperature, the scones are delicious. They go well with clotted cream and raspberry jam.

NUTRITIONAL INFORMATION: Calories: 351 kcal (per scone), Fat: 15g, Carbohydrates: 48g, Protein: 7g

DEHYDRATE

APPLE CHIPS

Prep Time 15 minutes	Cooking Time 4 hours	Servings 2

INGREDIENTS:

- 2 medium-sized apples
- 1 teaspoon lemon juice

INSTRUCTIONS:

1. Preheat the Ninja Woodfire Grill and Smoker to 50 degrees Celsius.
2. The apples should be washed and cored. Thinly slice them into 1/8-inch thick rounds.
3. To prevent browning, toss the apple slices in a bowl with lemon juice.
4. Arrange the apple slices in a single layer on the dehydrator racks, making sure they do not overlap.
5. Set the Ninja Woodfire Grill and Smoker to 50°C and place the racks inside.
6. Dehydrate the apple slices in the oven for 4-6 hours, or until crisp and dry.
7. Allow the apple chips to cool completely after removing them from the dehydrator.
8. For up to 2 weeks, store in an airtight container.

NUTRITIONAL INFORMATION:

Calories: 81, Carbohydrates: 22g, Fiber: 5g, Sugar: 14g, Fat: 1g, Protein: 1g

SPICY BEEF JERKY

Prep Time 4-24 hours	Cooking Time 3-4 hours	Servings 3

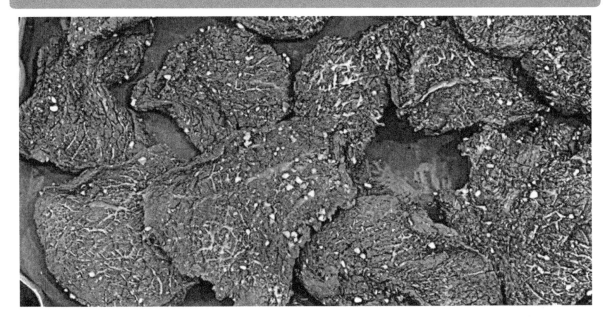

INGREDIENTS:

- 250g lean beef, thinly sliced
- 30ml soy sauce
- 1 tablespoons Worcestershire sauce
- 1/2 tablespoon liquid smoke
- 1/2 tablespoon brown sugar
- 1/2 teaspoon garlic powder
- 1/2 teaspoon onion powder
- 1/2 teaspoon paprika
- 1/3 teaspoon black pepper
- 1/3 teaspoon chili powder (adjust to taste)

INSTRUCTIONS:

1. Combine the soy sauce, Worcestershire sauce, liquid smoke, brown sugar, garlic powder, onion powder, paprika, black pepper, and chili powder in a mixing bowl. Combine thoroughly.

2. Add the thinly sliced beef to the marinade, making sure to coat all of the pieces. Refrigerate the bowl for 4-24 hours to allow the flavors to develop.

3. Preheat the Ninja Woodfire Grill and Smoker to 70 degrees Celsius.

4. Take the marinated beef out of the refrigerator and pat it dry with paper towels.

5. Place the beef slices on the dehydrator racks, leaving space between them.

6. Set the Ninja Woodfire Grill and Smoker to 70°C and place the racks inside.

7. Dehydrate the beef slices in the oven for 4-6 hours, or until dry and chewy.

8. Remove the jerky from the dehydrator and set it aside to cool completely before storing.

9. For up to 2 weeks, store in an airtight container.

NUTRITIONAL INFORMATION: Calories: 151, Carbohydrates: 5g, Fiber: 1g, Sugar: 4g, Fat: 3g, Protein: 22g

LEMON HERB KALE CHIPS

Prep Time 10 minutes	Cooking Time 2 hours	Servings 2

INGREDIENTS:

- 150g kale leaves, washed and dried
- 1 tablespoons olive oil
- 1/2 tablespoon lemon juice
- 1/2 teaspoon dried herbs (such as oregano, thyme, or rosemary)
- 1/3 teaspoon salt

INSTRUCTIONS:

1. Preheat the Ninja Woodfire Grill and Smoker to 60 degrees Celsius.

2. Take the kale leaves off the stems and tear them into bite-sized pieces.

3. Combine the olive oil, lemon juice, dried herbs, and salt in a large mixing bowl. Combine thoroughly.

4. Toss the kale leaves in the bowl with the oil mixture until evenly coated.

5. Arrange the kale leaves on the dehydrator racks in a single layer, not overlapping them.

6. Set the Ninja Woodfire Grill and Smoker to 60°C and place the racks inside.

7. Kale chips should be dehydrated for 2-4 hours, or until crispy and dry.

8. Allow the kale chips to cool in the dehydrator before serving.

9. For up to a week, store in an airtight container.

NUTRITIONAL INFORMATION: Calories: 83, Carbohydrates: 5g, Fiber: 1g, Sugar: 3g, Fat: 6g, Protein: 3g

MANGO SLICES WITH CHILI POWDER

Prep Time 10 minutes	Cooking Time 4-6 hours	Servings 2

INGREDIENTS:

- 1 large ripe mango
- 1 teaspoon chili powder (adjust to taste)

INSTRUCTIONS:

1. Preheat the Ninja Woodfire Grill and Smoker to 50 degrees Celsius.

2. Peel and cut the mangoes into thin slices about 1/4 inch thick.

3. Adjust the amount of chili powder sprinkled over the mango slices to your desired level of spiciness.

4. Place the mango slices on the dehydrator racks in a single layer, not touching each other.

5. Set the Ninja Woodfire Grill and Smoker to 50°C and place the racks inside.

6. Dehydrate the mango slices for 6-8 hours, or until they are slightly chewy but still dry.

7. Take the mango slices out of the dehydrator and set them aside to cool before serving.

8. For up to a week, store in an airtight container.

NUTRITIONAL INFORMATION: Calories: 81, Carbohydrates: 22g, Fiber: 3g, Sugar: 17g, Fat: 0g, Protein: 3g

CINNAMON SUGAR BANANA CHIPS

Prep Time 15 minutes	Cooking Time 4-5 hours	Servings 3

INGREDIENTS:

- 3 ripe bananas
- 1 tablespoon lemon juice
- 1 teaspoon ground cinnamon
- 1 tablespoon granulated sugar

INSTRUCTIONS:

1. Preheat the Ninja Woodfire Grill and Smoker to 50 degrees Celsius.
2. Peel and slice the bananas into thin rounds about 1/8 inch thick.
3. Combine lemon juice, ground cinnamon, and granulated sugar in a mixing bowl. Combine thoroughly.
4. Dip each banana slice in the cinnamon sugar mixture, coating both sides.
5. Place the coated banana slices on the dehydrator racks in a single layer, not touching one another.
6. Set the Ninja Woodfire Grill and Smoker to 50°C and place the racks inside.
7. Dehydrate the banana chips for 6 to 8 hours, or until crispy and dry.
8. Take the banana chips out of the dehydrator and set them aside to cool before serving.
9. For up to a week, store in an airtight container.

NUTRITIONAL INFORMATION: Calories: 92, Carbohydrates: 25g, Fiber: 5g, Sugar: 11g, Fat: 1g, Protein: 3g

TOMATO SLICES FOR SUN-DRIED TOMATOES

Prep Time 15 minutes	Cooking Time 10 hours	Servings 5

INGREDIENTS:

- 5 large ripe tomatoes
- Salt, to taste

INSTRUCTIONS:

1. Preheat the Ninja Woodfire Grill and Smoker to 50 degrees Celsius.
2. Wash the tomatoes and cut them into thin, 1/4-inch-thick slices.
3. Place the tomato slices on the dehydrator racks in a single layer, not touching each other.
4. Season the tomato slices with a pinch of salt.
5. Set the Ninja Woodfire Grill and Smoker to 50°C and place the racks inside.
6. Dehydrate the tomato slices for 8-10 hours, or until they are slightly chewy and dried.
7. Take the tomato slices out of the dehydrator and set them aside to cool before serving.
8. For up to 2 weeks, store in an airtight container.

NUTRITIONAL INFORMATION: Calories: 22, Carbohydrates: 4g, Fiber: 3g, Sugar: 2g, Fat: 1g, Protein: 2g

GARLIC AND HERB MUSHROOMS

Prep Time 10 minutes	Cooking Time 5 hours	Servings 2

INGREDIENTS:

- 300 grams fresh mushrooms (such as button or cremini)
- 1 tablespoons olive oil
- 1 cloves garlic, minced
- 1 teaspoon dried thyme
- 1 teaspoon dried rosemary
- Salt and pepper, to taste

INSTRUCTIONS:

1. Preheat the Ninja Woodfire Grill and Smoker to 60 degrees Celsius.

2. Clean the mushrooms and slice them thinly.

3. Combine olive oil, minced garlic, dried thyme, dried rosemary, salt, and pepper in a mixing bowl. Combine thoroughly.

4. Toss the mushroom slices in the bowl with the garlic and herb mixture to coat evenly.

5. Place the coated mushroom slices on the dehydrator racks in a single layer, not touching one another.

6. Set the Ninja Woodfire Grill and Smoker to 60°C and place the racks inside.

7. Dehydrate the mushrooms for 6-8 hours, or until completely dry and crisp.

8. Remove the mushroom slices from the dehydrator and place them in an airtight container to cool.

9. Use dehydrated mushrooms to add flavour to soups, stews, and sauces.

NUTRITIONAL INFORMATION: Calories: 82, Carbohydrates: 3g, Fiber: 2g, Sugar: 3g, Fat: 5g, Protein: 4g

ZESTY LEMON-LIME FRUIT LEATHER

Prep Time 10 minutes	Cooking Time 3 hours	Servings 3

INGREDIENTS:

- 2 large lemons
- 2 large limes
- 60 grams granulated sugar

INSTRUCTIONS:

1. Preheat the Ninja Woodfire Grill and Smoker to 50 degrees Celsius.

2. Juice the lemons and limes to yield about 250ml of juice.

3. Combine the lemon and lime juices with the granulated sugar in a saucepan. Stir constantly over medium-low heat until the sugar is completely dissolved.

4. Heat the mixture for another 2-3 minutes to slightly reduce the liquid.

5. Place the lemon-lime mixture on a baking sheet lined with parchment paper or a silicone baking mat. Spread it out evenly to create a thin layer.

6. Set the Ninja Woodfire Grill and Smoker to 50°C and place the baking sheet inside.

7. Dehydrate the fruit mixture for 4-6 hours, or until it is firm to the touch and no longer sticky.

8. Allow the fruit leather to cool after removing it from the dehydrator.

9. Roll the fruit leather into desired shapes and store in an airtight container.

NUTRITIONAL INFORMATION: Calories: 82, Carbohydrates: 22g, Fiber: 2g, Sugar: 17g, Fat: 1g, Protein: 2g

HERBS FOR HOMEMADE SEASONING BLENDS

Prep Time 15 minutes	Cooking Time 4-5 hours	Servings Varies

INGREDIENTS:

- Assorted fresh herbs (such as thyme, rosemary, oregano, basil, etc.)

INSTRUCTIONS:

1. Preheat the Ninja Woodfire Grill and Smoker to 50 degrees Celsius.

2. Wash and dry the fresh herbs thoroughly.

3. Discard the herb stems after removing the leaves.

4. Arrange the herb leaves on the dehydrator racks in a single layer.

5. Set the Ninja Woodfire Grill and Smoker to 50°C and place the racks inside.

6. Dehydrate the herb leaves in a dehydrator for 4-6 hours, or until completely dry and crumbly.

7. Allow the dried herb leaves to cool after removing them from the dehydrator.

8. To make homemade seasoning blends, crush the dried herb leaves with your hands or use a mortar and pestle.

9. Dehydrated herbs should be stored in an airtight container or spice jars for later use in recipes.

NUTRITIONAL INFORMATION: The nutritional value of dehydrated herbs varies depending on the herbs used. They are, however, low in calories and macronutrients because they are used in small amounts.

TERIYAKI BEEF BILTONG

Prep Time 10 minutes	Cooking Time 4-6 minutes	Servings 2

INGREDIENTS:

- 250 grams beef steak (such as sirloin or rump), thinly sliced
- 30 ml soy sauce
- 20 ml Worcestershire sauce
- 1/2 tablespoon brown sugar
- 1/2 teaspoon garlic powder
- 1/2 teaspoon ground ginger
- 1/2 teaspoon black pepper
- 1/2 teaspoon chilli flakes (optional)

INSTRUCTIONS:

1. Combine the soy sauce, Worcestershire sauce, brown sugar, garlic powder, ground ginger, black pepper, and chilli flakes (if using) in a mixing bowl. To make the teriyaki marinade, combine all of the ingredients in a mixing bowl.

2. Add the thinly sliced beef steak to the marinade, making sure to coat all of the slices. Allow it to marinate for at least 30 minutes or overnight for a more intense flavour.

3. Preheat the Ninja Woodfire Grill and Smoker to 50 degrees Celsius.

4. Allow any excess marinade to drip off the beef slices before removing them from the marinade.

5. Place the beef slices on the dehydrator racks in a single layer, not touching each other.

6. Set the Ninja Woodfire Grill and Smoker to 50°C and place the racks inside.

7. Dehydrate the beef slices for 8-10 hours, or until they're dry and chewy but still moist.

8. Remove the beef biltong from the dehydrator and place it in an airtight container to cool completely.

9. As a tasty high-protein snack, try the teriyaki beef biltong.

NUTRITIONAL INFORMATION: Calories: 202, Carbohydrates: 5g, Protein: 24g, Fat: 7g, Sodium: 905mg, Sugar: 4g

REHEAT

BBQ PULLED PORK SANDWICHES

Prep Time 15 minutes	Cooking Time 10-15 minutes	Servings 2

INGREDIENTS:

- 250 grams cooked and shredded pulled pork
- 120 ml BBQ sauce
- 2 burger buns
- Pickles, coleslaw, or other desired toppings

INSTRUCTIONS:

1. Preheat the Ninja Woodfire Grill and Smoker to 160°C on the "Reheat" setting.

2. Combine the shredded pulled pork and the BBQ sauce in a mixing bowl and mix well.

3. Place the pulled pork in an oven-safe dish or tray.

4. Close the lid on the Ninja Woodfire Grill and Smoker and place the dish or tray inside.

5. Allow the pulled pork to reheat for 15-20 minutes, or until thoroughly heated.

6. Lightly toast the burger buns on the grill while the pulled pork reheats.

7. Remove the toasted buns and pulled pork from the Ninja Woodfire Grill and Smoker.

8. Place a generous amount of the reheated pulled pork on the bottom bun and assemble the pulled pork sandwiches.

9. Pickles, coleslaw, or other desired toppings can be added on top.

10. Serve the sandwich with the top bun immediately.

NUTRITIONAL INFORMATION: The nutritional information will differ depending on the ingredients and brands used.

GRILLED CHICKEN QUESADILLAS

Prep Time 10 minutes	Cooking Time 10 minutes	Servings 2

INGREDIENTS:

- 1-2 large tortilla wraps
- 200 grams cooked and shredded grilled chicken
- 60 grams shredded cheddar cheese
- 1 small red onion, thinly sliced
- 1 small red bell pepper, thinly sliced
- 1/2 small green bell pepper, thinly sliced
- 1/2 tsp ground cumin
- 1/2 tsp chili powder
- Salt and pepper to taste
- Sour cream and salsa for serving

INSTRUCTIONS:

1. Preheat the Ninja Woodfire Grill and Smoker to 160°C on the "Reheat" setting.

2. Combine the shredded grilled chicken, ground cumin, chili powder, salt, and pepper in a mixing bowl. Coat the chicken with the mixture.

3. Lay the tortilla wraps out on a clean surface.

4. Distribute the shredded chicken, sliced red onion, sliced red and green bell peppers, and shredded cheddar cheese evenly on one half of each tortilla.

5. Fold the tortilla in half to cover the filling and gently press the edges together to seal.

6. Place the quesadillas on a baking dish or tray that is oven-safe.

7. Close the lid on the Ninja Woodfire Grill and Smoker and place the dish or tray inside.

8. Allow the quesadillas to reheat for about 10-15 minutes, or until the cheese melts and the filling is thoroughly heated.

9. Allow the quesadillas to cool for a few minutes after removing them from the Ninja Woodfire Grill and Smoker.

10. Serve each quesadilla in wedges with sour cream and salsa on the side.

NUTRITIONAL INFORMATION: The nutritional information will differ depending on the ingredients and brands used.

SMOKED BRISKET TACOS

Prep Time 15 minutes	Cooking Time 20 minutes	Servings 6

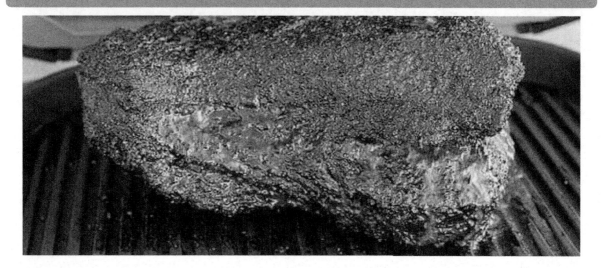

INGREDIENTS:

- 700 grams smoked brisket, cooked and shredded

- 10 small flour or corn tortillas
- 2 small red onion, finely chopped

- 2 small bunch fresh cilantro, chopped
- 2 lime, cut into wedges
- Hot sauce, to taste
- Salt and pepper, to taste

INSTRUCTIONS:

1. Preheat the Ninja Woodfire Grill and Smoker to 160°C on the "Reheat" setting.
2. In an oven-safe dish or tray, place the shredded brisket.
3. Close the lid on the Ninja Woodfire Grill and Smoker and place the dish or tray inside.
4. Allow the brisket to reheat for 10-15 minutes, or until thoroughly heated.
5. Warm the tortillas on the grill for a few seconds on each side while the brisket reheats.
6. The brisket and tortillas should be removed from the Ninja Woodfire Grill and Smoker.
7. Place a portion of the reheated brisket on each tortilla to make the tacos.
8. Sprinkle with chopped red onion, fresh cilantro, lime juice, and hot sauce to taste.
9. Season with salt and pepper to taste.
10. Serve the tacos right away.

NUTRITIONAL INFORMATION: The nutritional information will differ depending on the specific ingredients and brands used.

HONEY GLAZED HAM WITH PINEAPPLE SALSA

Prep Time 10 minutes	Cooking Time 10 minutes	Servings 2

INGREDIENTS:

- 250 grams cooked ham, sliced
- 30 ml honey
- 20 ml Dijon mustard
- 1/2 small pineapple, peeled and diced
- 1/2 small red bell pepper, diced
- 1/2 small red onion, diced
- 1/2 small bunch fresh cilantro, chopped
- Juice of 1 lime
- Salt and pepper, to taste

INSTRUCTIONS:

1. Preheat the Ninja Woodfire Grill and Smoker to 160°C on the "Reheat" setting.
2. In a small mixing bowl, combine the honey and Dijon mustard.

3. Glaze the sliced ham with the honey mustard mixture.

4. Place the glazed ham slices on a baking dish or tray that is oven-safe.

5. Close the lid on the Ninja Woodfire Grill and Smoker and place the dish or tray inside.

6. Allow the ham to reheat for about 10-15 minutes, or until thoroughly heated.

7. While the ham is reheating, make the pineapple salsa in a separate bowl by combining diced pineapple, red bell pepper, red onion, chopped cilantro, lime juice, salt, and pepper. Combine thoroughly.

8. Allow the ham to rest for a few minutes after removing it from the Ninja Woodfire Grill and Smoker.

9. Serve the reheated ham slices alongside the pineapple salsa.

NUTRITIONAL INFORMATION: The nutritional information will differ depending on the ingredients and brands used.

SMOKY BEEF CHILI

Prep Time 15 minutes	Cooking Time 20 minutes	Servings 6

INGREDIENTS:

- 600 grams cooked beef chili
- 2 small onion, chopped
- 2 small bell pepper, chopped
- 500 grams diced tomatoes
- 280 ml beef broth
- 3 cloves garlic, minced

- 30 ml chili powder
- 7 ml ground cumin
- Salt and pepper, to taste
- Optional toppings: grated cheese, sour cream, chopped cilantro

INSTRUCTIONS:

1. Preheat the Ninja Woodfire Grill and Smoker to 160°C on the "Reheat" setting.

2. Heat the cooked beef chili in a large saucepan over medium heat until thoroughly heated.

3. While the chili is heating up, soften the onion and bell pepper in a separate pan.

4. Reheat the chili with the sautéed onion and bell pepper.

5. Combine the diced tomatoes, beef broth, minced garlic, chili powder, and ground cumin in a mixing bowl.

6. Season to taste with salt and pepper.

7. Allow the chili to simmer, stirring occasionally, for about 10-15 minutes.

8. Reheated smoky beef chili should be served in bowls.

9. Optional garnishes include grated cheese, sour cream, and chopped cilantro.

NUTRITIONAL INFORMATION: The nutritional information will differ depending on the ingredients and brands used.

GRILLED VEGETABLE STIR-FRY

Prep Time 15 minutes	Cooking Time 20 minutes	Servings 6

INGREDIENTS:

- 700 grams leftover grilled vegetables (such as bell peppers, zucchini, eggplant, etc.)
- 2 small onion, sliced
- 3 cloves garlic, minced
- 20 ml soy sauce
- 20 ml sesame oil
- 6 ml rice vinegar
- 7 ml honey
- Salt and pepper, to taste
- Optional garnish: sesame seeds, chopped green onions

INSTRUCTIONS:

1. Preheat the Ninja Woodfire Grill and Smoker to 160°C on the "Reheat" setting.

2. Warm a small amount of oil in a large skillet over medium heat.

3. Sauté the sliced onion and minced garlic in the skillet until softened.

4. Stir in the leftover grilled vegetables for a few minutes, or until heated through.

5. In a small mixing bowl, combine the soy sauce, sesame oil, rice vinegar, and honey.

6. Stir the sauce into the vegetables in the skillet to coat.

7. Season to taste with salt and pepper.

8. Stir-fry for an additional 2-3 minutes.

9. Remove the skillet from the heat and set aside for a few minutes to allow the vegetables to cool.

10. Reheated grilled vegetable stir-fry should be served in bowls.

11. Optional garnishes include sesame seeds and chopped green onions.

NUTRITIONAL INFORMATION: The nutritional information will differ depending on the ingredients and brands used.

SMOKED SALMON AND CREAM CHEESE BAGELS

Prep Time 10 minutes	Cooking Time 10 minutes	Servings 4

INGREDIENTS:

- 4 bagels, sliced in half
- 250 grams smoked salmon
- 120 grams cream cheese
- 2 small red onion, thinly sliced
- Capers, for garnish
- Fresh dill, for garnish

INSTRUCTIONS:

1. Preheat the Ninja Woodfire Grill and Smoker to 160°C on the "Reheat" setting.

2. Reheat the bagel halves directly on the grill grate for about 3 minutes, or until lightly toasted.

3. Spread the cream cheese evenly on each half of the bagel.

4. Smoked salmon slices should be placed on top of the cream cheese.

5. Return the bagel halves to the grill grate and reheat for another 2 minutes.

6. Remove from the grill and serve with thinly sliced red onion, capers, and fresh dill on the side.

7. Serve the smoked salmon and cream cheese bagels right away.

NUTRITIONAL INFORMATION: The nutritional information will differ depending on the ingredients and brands used.

BARBECUE RIBS WITH TANGY SAUCE

Prep Time 10 minutes	Cooking Time 15 minutes	Servings 4

INGREDIENTS:

- 550 grams leftover barbecue ribs
- 150 ml barbecue sauce
- 40 ml apple cider vinegar
- 25 ml Worcestershire sauce
- 25 ml honey
- Salt and pepper, to taste

INSTRUCTIONS:

1. Preheat the Ninja Woodfire Grill and Smoker to 160°C on the "Reheat" setting.

2. Combine the barbecue sauce, apple cider vinegar, Worcestershire sauce, and honey in a small saucepan.

3. Cook, stirring occasionally, until the sauce is heated through.

4. Reheat the leftover barbecue ribs on the grill grate for about 5 minutes.

5. Brush the ribs with the prepared tangy sauce while they are reheating.

6. Continue to reheat for 5 minutes, or until the ribs are thoroughly heated.

7. Remove from the grill and season to taste with salt and pepper.

8. Serve the reheated barbecue ribs with the tangy sauce on the side.

NUTRITIONAL INFORMATION: The nutritional information will differ depending on the ingredients and brands used.

SMOKED SAUSAGE AND PEPPERS SANDWICHES

Prep Time 15 minutes	Cooking Time 10 minutes	Servings 6

INGREDIENTS:

- 6 smoked sausages
- 2 red bell pepper, sliced
- 1 green bell pepper, sliced
- 2 onion, sliced

- 3 tablespoons olive oil
- Salt and pepper, to taste
- 6 hoagie rolls

INSTRUCTIONS:

1. Preheat the Ninja Woodfire Grill and Smoker to 160°C on the "Reheat" setting.

2. Grill the smoked sausages, bell peppers, and onion slices over medium heat.

3. Drizzle with olive oil and season with salt and pepper to taste.

4. Reheat for 5 minutes, or until the sausages are thoroughly heated and the vegetables are tender.

5. While the sausages and vegetables are reheating, split the hoagie rolls and toast them for 2 minutes on the grill grate.

6. Take the sausages and vegetables off the grill and place them in the hoagie rolls.

7. Serve the smoked sausage and peppers sandwiches right away.

NUTRITIONAL INFORMATION: The nutritional information will differ depending on the specific ingredients and brands used.

GRILLED STEAK FAJITAS

Prep Time 15 minutes	Cooking Time 10-15 minutes	Servings 6

INGREDIENTS:

- 600 grams leftover grilled steak, sliced
- 1 1/2 red bell pepper, sliced
- 1 1/2 green bell pepper, sliced
- 1 onion, sliced
- 3 tablespoons olive oil
- 1 1/2 tablespoon chili powder
- 1 1/2 teaspoon ground cumin
- 1 1/2 teaspoon paprika
- Salt and pepper, to taste
- 5 large tortillas
- Optional toppings: guacamole, sour cream, salsa, shredded cheese

INSTRUCTIONS:

1. Preheat the Ninja Woodfire Grill and Smoker to 160°C on the "Reheat" setting.

2. Place the grilled steak slices, bell pepper slices, and onion slices on the grill grate.

3. Sprinkle with chili powder, cumin, paprika, salt, and pepper and drizzle with olive oil.

4. Reheat for 5 minutes, or until the steak is thoroughly heated and the vegetables are tender.

5. Wrap the tortillas in foil and place them on the grill grate to warm for 2 minutes while the steak and vegetables reheat.

6. Take the steak and vegetables off the grill and place them in the warm tortillas.

7. Reheated grilled steak fajitas can be topped with guacamole, sour cream, salsa, and shredded cheese.

NUTRITIONAL INFORMATION: The nutritional information will differ depending on the specific ingredients and brands used.

CONCLUSION

Congratulations on finishing the "Ninja Woodfire Outdoor Grill and Smoker Cookbook" culinary journey! We hope this cookbook has inspired you to try your hand at woodfire cooking with your Ninja Woodfire Grill and Smoker.

We've shared a variety of delectable recipes in this book, from juicy grilled steaks to smoky pulled pork and delectable desserts. We've also given you valuable insights into the techniques, tips, and tricks that will help you become a woodfire cooking master.

You should now have a better understanding of the history and tradition of woodfire grilling and smoking. You've learned about the advantages of using the Ninja Woodfire Grill and Smoker, and you're armed with the necessary tools and safety precautions to ensure a safe cooking environment.

You've investigated the various types of wood and charcoal, learning how they can impart distinct flavours to your dishes. You've also mastered the techniques of searing, smoking, tenderizing, resting, and carving, which are all necessary for perfect results.

We hope this cookbook has sparked your interest in woodfire cooking and inspired you to cook memorable meals for your family and friends. The Ninja Woodfire Grill and Smoker's versatility and capabilities are limitless, allowing you to experiment and push the boundaries of your culinary creativity.

Remember to enjoy yourself and the process of woodfire cooking. The smoky aromas, sizzle of the grill, and satisfaction of serving a perfectly prepared meal are all part of the experience. So, gather your loved ones, turn on your Ninja Woodfire Grill and Smoker, and set out on a culinary adventure that will leave you with lasting memories.

Thank you for your interest in the "Ninja Woodfire Outdoor Grill and Smoker Cookbook." As you continue to explore the art of woodfire cooking, we wish you many delightful moments and delicious meals. Enjoy your grilling and smoking!

Printed in Great Britain
by Amazon